AUSTRALIAN BIBLIOGRAPHY

AUSTRALIAN BIBLIOGRAPHY

A Guide to Printed Sources of Information

D. H. BORCHARDT

M.A., DIP.N.Z.LIB.SCH., A.L.A., F.L.A.A.

Chief Librarian, La Trobe University, Melbourne

F. W. CHESHIRE

Melbourne Canberra Sydney

Library of Congress Catalog Card No. 66 - 18017

COPYRIGHT

First published 1963
Second Edition revised and enlarged 1966
by F. W. Cheshire Pty Ltd
338 Little Collins Street, Melbourne
Garema Place, Canberra
and 142 Victoria Road, Marrickville, N.S.W.

Printed in Australia
by The Hawthorn Press, Melbourne

Registered in Australia
for transmission by post as a book

"Ich möchte wohl den Titel des
letzten Buches wissen, das
gedruckt werden wird."
G. C. LICHTENBERG

PREFACE

This book is designed to be an introduction to the printed bibliography of things Australian. As potential users I have had in mind the undergraduate university student, the student of librarianship in Australian libraries and the general reader who may care to be properly informed on Australian sources of information. I have preferred as much as possible to draw attention to bibliographic work properly conceived as such. Unfortunately, there is no welter of material to choose from and in some important areas of scholarship there exist to date no bibliographies of Australian writings. Indeed, I found it necessary on several occasions to cite bibliographies appended to one scholarly work or another as if they were bibliographies compiled with the intent of presenting a balanced overall view—which, with all respect to many authors, they do not usually present. But in the absence of any bibliographic survey, a well-chosen list of references appended to a reliable work of research can be a good substitute. On the other hand, I have excluded mere indices to periodicals as these are not bibliographies in any sense of the word. The Trust Territories and Dependencies of the Commonwealth of Australia have also been deliberately omitted from this survey.

I am indebted to my colleague Mr G. D. Richardson, Principal Librarian of the Public Library of New South Wales, for much valued criticism. To my friend Assoc. Professor J. A. Cardno I owe thanks for preserving me from falling into some linguistic pitfalls, and to Miss M. Carter for giving unstintedly of her time to complete the typing.

Some of the material here presented has already been briefly treated in a recent contribution to *College and research libraries* (v23, 1962) under the title *Australian bibliography: an assay*. I am obliged to the editor of that journal for permission to repeat a few brief sections here.

May 1963

PREFACE TO THE SECOND EDITION

The demand for a new edition of this Guide after only three years is gratifying. I have availed myself of this opportunity of correcting errors and of adding references to over 50 bibliographies most of which have appeared since 1963, and to record changes where they have occurred in several bibliographies. It is indeed pleasing to note that there has been a considerable increase in bibliographic activities in Australia during the past three years. Though I have mentioned the more significant additions only, there can be no doubt that many of my colleagues are active in the development of bibliographic guides to sources of information in Australia.

I am grateful to those of my colleagues who have taken the trouble of pointing out possible improvements, and particularly to Mr G. D. Richardson who kindly read through the typescript and offered critical comments, and to Miss M. J. Hagger, Head, School of Librarianship, RMIT, Melbourne; Mr B. Reid of the State Library of Victoria, and Mr T. Triffitt, of the University of Tasmania Library, who helped to locate information at a time when I was fairly busy with many other commitments.

I wish to thank Mrs M. Harari for having generously assisted with the proof reading of both the first and the second edition.

Melbourne   D.H.B.
March 1966

CONTENTS

I   *Introduction*   1

II   *Library Catalogues and General Retrospective Bibliographies*   3

III   *Current National Bibliographies and Indices to Newspapers*   11

IV   *Bibliographies of Subject Areas*   18

V   *Regional Bibliography*   48

VI   *Government Publications*   53

VII   *Bibliography in Australia*   60

VIII   *List of Works Referred to*   70

SUBJECT INDEX   93

I

INTRODUCTION

Ever since European sailors of many nations went searching for that land mass which — in the opinion of many ancient geographers — was necessary to keep the earth in balance, even though nobody seems to have given much thought to the pivot, Terra Australis has been the source or object of sagas, utopias, adventure stories, missionary accounts, romances, poems, histories true and false. Though its discovery proper and subsequent annexation by West-European civilization occurred much later than was the case with all other substantial inhabited land areas, this delayed entry into the world of letters was compensated by an increased spread of literacy, a greater prolixity of writers and a considerable improvement in the spread of printing. It is not unnatural, therefore, that there is a larger body of printed references to the early history of Australia than to that of other countries at similar stages of development.

Nevertheless, books and articles about Australia fall almost naturally into two classes, divided by that same line which marks the transition from the encyclopædic to the specialist approach to knowledge in the nineteenth century. Most writings on Australia before the middle of the nineteenth century are of the omnibus kind, including historico-political as well as social *and* scientific treatments of the whole continent — or at least of such parts of it as were known at the time. But in the middle of the nineteenth century, Western civilization experienced changes in its general scientific outlook and developed new approaches to social problems which affected all scholarly as well as entertainment writing — changes which perhaps not quite haphazardly coincided with political developments in Australia and which, in turn, helped in the establishment of the long-hoped-for responsible government in the Australian colonies.

The growth and development of Australia's national consciousness was at once cause and effect of political adolescence and subsequent maturity, the beginning of native trends in the pure

1

sciences, in sociological thought and even in arts and letters during the second half of the nineteenth century; it also brought plenty of material for literary craftsmen of all kinds.

As early as 1866 we find an essay on Australian bibliography written by J. E. Tenison Woods, and published under that title in two instalments in the *Australian monthly magazine*.[164] Though Woods is mainly concerned with the first references to Australia in the reports of voyages made by European sailors in the sixteenth century, he makes some very pertinent remarks on the carelessness of some historians and on the excessive verbiage behind which facts are often hidden. Woods' interpretation of the word "bibliography" may differ from that of our time, but his essay is an interesting early contribution to Australian historiography and bibliography in general.

In selecting from the fairly sizeable — but by no means vast — volume of bibliographies on things and matters Australian, I have endeavoured to single out the more important ones and to assess briefly their significance. Historiography and sociography have changed during the past five decades. Even as recently as in the nineteen-thirties a scholar could and would unblushingly present a piece of research and original thought without going to the trouble of listing at the end of his book the sources which he had consulted. This is scarcely done today owing to various influences, mainly those of the universities of the USA, where this "old-fashioned" method of presenting scholarly work without citations of background literature had been in almost complete abeyance since the end of the First World War. Not for them Nietzsche's warning: "Sieh hinaus, sieh nicht zurück; man geht zu Grunde, wenn man immer zu den Gründen geht". But I do not wish to decry the new fashion. It has its virtues — indeed, it is but a concomitant of a time when printing presses work at such a rate of production that a librarian cannot help feeling like the sorcerer's apprentice.

II

LIBRARY CATALOGUES AND
GENERAL RETROSPECTIVE BIBLIOGRAPHIES

A. *Library Catalogues*

There is a clear and proper distinction between library catalogues and subject bibliographies; the former describe collections of books housed under one roof, the latter describe printed matter which has some common denominator. Given favourable circumstances, a library catalogue could in effect be a subject bibliography, and in the case of some rather narrowly defined subjects this is quite feasible. But the subject "Australia" is certainly not in the category of such small subject areas, and libraries which have specialized in collecting Australiana for some decades would find the publication of their catalogue a large and expensive undertaking. It is therefore not surprising that no such library catalogue has been issued for many years.

The collection of Australiana by private persons is today more common than earlier in the century, but compared with the wealth that has been spent on the collecting of other subjects, e.g., Americana, history of medicine, and others, the private fortunes used for the purpose of collecting books on Australia have been rather small.

When we look for any of the more noteworthy collections formed outside Australia, we note in the first instance that none of them deal exclusively with Australia. Indeed, the only two substantial printed catalogues of libraries containing large sections of Australiana are the York Gate Library and the Royal Commonwealth Society's Library, both of which are collections dealing with the history and development of the British Commonwealth. The York Gate Library was collected by Stephen William Silver of London, and a *Catalogue*[135] of the collection was first issued in 1882. In the introduction to the second edition (1886), the compiler, Edward A. Petherick, states that the York Gate Library "now contains nearly 5000 volumes and pamphlets, in-

3

cluding many early productions of the colonial press". The hand-somely produced volume suggests a bigger library, but bulk has been achieved by exhaustive indexing of the great collections of voyages. The sections dealing specifically with Australia comprise pp. 234-271; within each section the entries are arranged chrono-logically except for titles of pamphlets which are gathered at the end.

The fate of private collections, once the *spiritus movendi* (or should it be *collocandi?*) has disappeared, depends on many different factors. One of the famous collectors of Australiana, Edward Augustus Petherick, whose career as a bibliographer, bookseller and agent was varied and at times distressing, had to sell his own library of 15,000 volumes to the Commonwealth National Library in 1911 without having been able to get his "Bibliography of Australasia" published. Other collectors pre-ferred to let their libraries be distributed to the four corners of the earth through auction sales, so that the catalogues of auction-eers and booksellers are sometimes the only records of their collecting activities. These catalogues are usually very well pro-duced and represent descriptive bibliographies of high quality — well-known examples are Francis Edwards Ltd. *Australasian cata-logues*[74] [with varying subtitles] of 1899, 1928, 1934 (Partington Collection), and 1936.

The fortunes of the British overseas during the past 200 years are reflected — and not without glory — in the simple changes of name of one of Britain's famous institutions: The Royal Common-wealth Society, known until 1928 as the Royal Colonial Institute, and then until 1958 as the Royal Empire Society. From the bibliographer's point of view it was most active during the nine-teen-thirties when its library was under the direction of the able and far-sighted Percy Evans Lewis. With financial help from the Carnegie United Kingdom Trust and from the Carnegie Cor-poration of New York, the Society was able to publish its *Subject catalogue of the library*,[130] in four volumes, between 1930 and 1937; the compiler was Evans Lewis. The second volume records "publications relating to the southern hemisphere outside the African region"; entries are not limited to books and pamphlets, but include references to articles in journals, papers read before learned societies and analytics for books of essays. The Australian section and the accounts of voyages in this second volume cover over 400 pages and no student of Australia can get far without being thoroughly familiar with this bibliographic catalogue of one of the best collections on the subject outside Australia.

Another British institution, the Institute of Commonwealth Studies, London — much younger than the Royal Commonwealth Society and established principally to assist research workers who have come to London to pursue specific studies of the British Commonwealth of Nations — published a useful guide to Australian and other reference material available in Great Britain. The Institute has not a very large library of its own and the work of its then Librarian, A. R. Hewitt, *Guide to resources for Commonwealth studies in London, Oxford and Cambridge, with bibliographical and other information,* 1957,[94] is of great help to the Institute's workers and is also to date the only bibliography of Commonwealth bibliographies. Despite its limitation to material available in the three centres named in the title, it contains a wealth of references, and within the compass of the large field which Hewitt covers, Australian bibliographies and sources are adequately though not exhaustively represented. Hewitt's *Guide* describes the collections of the important public and private libraries of the region, the general contents of archival collections, including the Public Records Office, and also lists library resources by subjects. The emphasis is on history and the social sciences.

Though Australia cannot by any standards be considered a library-conscious country, the wealthier states established libraries of a sort fairly early. Towards the end of the nineteenth century the public libraries of Sydney and Melbourne and the libraries serving the legislatures of these states contained respectable collections, and some of these were indeed remarkable for their time. One of these, the Free Public Library in Sydney, now better known as the Public Library of New South Wales, saw fit to commemorate the centennial of the foundation of the colony of New South Wales by the publication of the *Australasian bibliography . . . Catalogue of books in the Free Public Library, Sydney, relating to, or published in, Australasia.*[113] This remarkably early effort was completed in 1893 and consists of three parts: alphabetical list of authors, authors arranged under areas, and a classified subject and title catalogue with a general index to all subjects. It represents the first serious attempt at an Australian bibliography compiled in Australia. The classified subject and title catalogue, which forms the third section, contains a brief "Guide to the shelves" with the library's classification system which, to a layman, may seem more sensible than the system later imposed upon this excellent collection. As a source of information, the *Australasian bibliography* of 1893 has not outlived its usefulness even today; it is one of the few reliable guides to publications of the second half of the nineteenth century.

Another great library, the State Library of Victoria, tried to provide a guide to the Australiana in its collection. T. F. Cooke's *Classified catalogue of Australiana in the Public Lending Library of Victoria* [161] was issued in 1936. In his preface E. R. Pitt points out that about one-tenth of the Library's 70,000 volumes can be legitimately considered of special Australian interest. The catalogue is arranged according to the Dewey Decimal Classification, but the entries are bibliographically quite inadequate; indeed, even the date of publication is given only in "the sections relating to Australian and New Zealand discovery, travel and description, and to Australian and New Zealand history . . . as a guide to students". The possibility of serious study in other fields was apparently not seriously considered. Users of this somewhat amateurish catalogue should also note that biography and fiction are listed at the very end of the classed arrangement and not under their respective Decimal Classification numbers. There are no annotations.

On a much smaller scale is Currie's *A catalogue of books on Australia and the neighbouring colonies* [68a] which is based on his own library. Its standard of bibliographic entry is poor and though the *Catalogue* comprises 144 numbered pages, many of these are blank — presumably for "future additions" — all entries are repeated, first in an alphabetical sequence and then in an arrangement under each colony. The Currie collection is now housed in the State Library of Victoria.

B. *General Retrospective Bibliographies*

Even in the comparatively limited field of Australiana, library catalogues must necessarily be limited. Collections formed some fifty or more years ago — when it may have been still possible to acquire all printed material on Australia, at least from 1788 onward — are, of course, deficient in the recent literature; yet it has become not only very costly but also difficult to form comprehensive collections during the last two to three decades owing to the scarcity of many significant works. We shall therefore turn our attention from library catalogues to bibliographies which, though still insufficient in coverage as well as in depth, offer some guidance to the printed sources on Australia.

Bibliographies on Australia — as on any other subject — can be divided into groups or classes according to their scope, their form, their limitations of one kind or another. For the present purpose they will be arranged into several major groups: general retrospective bibliographies dealing with Australia as a whole; current bibliographies; regional bibliographies; subject bibliographies on various aspects of Australian culture and civilization; and bibliographies on Australian government publications.

There exist, in addition, a few bibliographies of bibliographies which it will be necessary and useful to list by way of introduction. None of these are descriptive guides to Australian reference material and even the most comprehensive of these efforts is mainly a list of entries without commentary: *Australian bibliography and bibliographical services*,[34] compiled by the Bibliographical Centre of the Australian Advisory Council on Bibliographical Services (AACOBS) in 1960. The title of this useful work is rather misleading as there is no description or even mention of such services in Australia. However, the work lists 1289 titles of bibliographies of one sort or another as well as 78 provisional titles of bibliographic work in progress at the time of printing (1960). In fact, *Australian bibliography and bibliographical services* presents the basic bibliographical aids of the Centre in print, and as such records the "state of the bibliographic art" in Australia at a certain period of time. The picture is rather stark: black and white lines criss-cross and there is no shading. Yet it will, for many years, remain the corner-stone which all present and future bibliographers will have to incorporate in their work.

In response to questionnaires from the UNESCO Division of Libraries, Documentation and Archives and as a document for presentation to AACOBS, the Australian Bibliographical Centre prepared a number of reports on bibliographical and library activities in Australia. Since 1961 these reports have been named *National bibliographical service and related activities*[34b] and have appeared biennially, recording information on the organization of libraries and archives in Australia, on professional activities and on bibliographical work completed or in progress. The reports are set out as answers to the UNESCO questionnaire and no attempt is made to go beyond the limits set by this international document. It is nevertheless a useful supplement to *Australian bibliography and bibliographical services,* especially because it does give some information on services.

Some less comprehensive lists of bibliographies have occasionally been compiled by individuals or institutions, e.g., the Mitchell Library's *Selected list of reference books for Australasia and the Antarctic,* 1954,[119] a brief list of 16 pages. It is rightly called a "preliminary list" but it contains a number of interesting and useful entries which are not to be found in *Australian bibliography and bibliographical services.* The National Library of Australia issued a *Select list of bibliographical publications relating to Australia*[33] in 1951, and an unnamed compiler produced *A selected list of bibliographical aids covering the Pacific region, Australia and New Zealand*[132] in 1952, in which 159 items are cited. The majority of these and similar lists contain, of course, identical references with rare additions of one or two specialized sources of information. Unfortunately, quite a few entries are so general and broad that they are not likely to produce specific information on Australian bibliography. A brief essay on the more important items of the bibliography of Australia, by D. H. Borchardt,[53] appeared in *College & research libraries,* v23, 1962, where fifty titles are discussed and listed.

Outstanding among the retrospective bibliographies on Australia which cover the early period of settlement and have no subject limitations is Sir John Ferguson's monumental *Bibliography of Australia, 1784-1900,* 1941-1961[81]* which will ever remain the basis for bibliographic research on Australia. The product of years of meticulous study, not only by the compiler, but also by scores of librarians and bibliographers who helped in the verification of titles, it offers more complete information on Australian books, pamphlets, broadsides and the like than any other bibliography at present available. The scope of the work is described in the introduction to the first volume, and the principles of selection applied by the compiler are reiterated in the introduction to the third volume. These limitations must be borne in mind when using the *Bibliography of Australia.* In particular the user should note that entries in volumes 1-4 covering the years 1784 to 1850, are arranged in chronological order, while

* At the time of writing, Volume 7 is scheduled to appear late in 1966.

volumes 5-7 show entries in alphabetical order of authors. It must also be noted that in the later volumes duplication of entry has occurred on more than one occasion, due perhaps to the fact that many hands have helped in listing the quite considerable number of works published between 1845 and 1900. Most entries are accompanied by a descriptive note and a reference to the location of at least one copy. The first four volumes have an author and subject index and volume 7 will contain a subject index to the period 1851-1900 described in volumes 5 to 7.

There are numerous examples of less important bibliographies of Australia as a whole. As Ferguson's work now commands an extraordinarily high price on the book market, some of the lesser bibliographic efforts are frequently acquired to serve the need of research. For example, S. A. Spence's *A bibliography of selected early books and pamphlets relating to Australia, 1610-1880,* 1952,[142] and its supplement, covering the years 1881-1900, issued in 1955. The two parts contain some 1800-odd entries, including a useful but very brief list of early Australian engraved portraits. The compiler's claim that it was his "first consideration . . . to obtain material which, up to the present, has failed to appear in any single volume relating to Australia" would seem somewhat exaggerated.

A useful bibliography of "Australian Life" was compiled during the war by the Bibliography Division of the Library of Congress: *A select list of references on Australia,* 1942.[155] The list is arranged according to subject areas and contains 793 items most of which are held by the Library of Congress. While the list is not claimed to be exhaustive it presents a fair sample of the more significant writings on Australia.

A more specialized type of general bibliography is represented by the attempts of L. L. Politzer to list foreign language references in a number of pamphlets: *Bibliography of Dutch literature on Australia,* 1953[123]; *Bibliography of French literature on Australia, 1595-1946,* 1952[124]; *Bibliography of German literature on Australia, 1700-1947,* 1952.[125]

Before leaving the area of retrospective bibliographies, mention must be made of the excellent work by A. B. Foxcroft, *The Australian catalogue,* 1911.[83] The subtitle "A reference index to the books and periodicals published and still current in the Commonwealth of Australia" clearly describes its scope. A special feature of the *Australian catalogue* is a list of government publications then in print. The fact that it has been reprinted by H. Pordes in 1961 is an indication of the usefulness of this catalogue. Indeed, it is an early attempt at a national bibliography of Australia and it was not until 1933 that the project was again tackled on a proper scale.

III

CURRENT NATIONAL BIBLIOGRAPHIES
AND INDICES TO NEWSPAPERS

A. *Australian National Bibliography*

The compilation of a current national bibliography is indeed a fairly recent achievement in Australia. Though the output of Australian commercial publishers has, until now, not been large (765 titles in 1958 and 531 titles in 1961), the government printers of the States and of the Commonwealth have been producing vast masses of printed matter for many years. The problem of bibliographic control of government publications will be discussed in detail in a later chapter; here it suffices to say that government publications are now included in the *Australian national bibliography*.[44] A national bibliography may justifiably also include books on the country as well as books by nationals published abroad. Such an extension of the concept of national bibliography may have a slightly chauvinistic ring about it, but in a country with a comparatively small population (and consequently a small literary market) many writers naturally try to find publishers abroad.

The first *Annual catalogue of Australian publications*[25] was issued by the Commonwealth National Library in 1937. It covered publications which had appeared in 1936 and had been deposited in the Commonwealth Parliamentary Library in pursuance of Section 40 of the Copyright Act (1912); it excluded government publications of the Commonwealth and the States, but these were included from the second volume — 1938 — onwards. The war years prevented any extension of the coverage of this bibliography but in 1946 it became possible to satisfy demands for prompter listings of Australian books by the publication of a monthly list *Books published in Australia*.[28] This list was expanded and improved in 1952 by a second monthly publication, *Australian government publications*.[42] Both lists were cumulated annually in the *Annual catalogue of Australian publi-*

cations.[25] The National Library also issues an annual list of selected references under the title *Australian books.*[26] The series began in 1933 as *Select list of representative works dealing with Australia* and is in effect a reprint of a list appended to the *Official yearbook of the Commonwealth of Australia;* the title was changed in 1949. These lists give authors and titles of books and titles of periodicals classified into broad groups; within each section entries are divided into two sub-groups "Standard works in print" and "Recent publications of interest". Wherever possible, prices are given. The entries are not limited to books dealing with Australia but include important books on other subjects written by Australians. The series *Australian books* incorporates therefore many of the entries of the *Australian national bibliography* to which are added those older titles which are considered to be sufficiently important. *Australian books* is a useful and pleasantly produced publication — a little on the national advertising side, but not too much so.

The passing of the National Library Act (1961) by the Commonwealth Parliament provided a suitable occasion to reorganize and improve the existing national bibliographies. The *Annual catalogue,* of which 25 issues had appeared, and the two monthly lists of Australian publications all ceased in December 1960. Since January 1961 the National Library of Australia has begun to issue on a monthly basis the *Australian national bibliography*[44] which is cumulated into an annual volume with the same title. The monthly issues include books published in Australia, books by Australian residents published abroad and books on Australia published overseas restricted in the main to books in the English language. Entries are arranged alphabetically by author; there is a subject and title index, and a classification number — based on the sixteenth edition of the Dewey Decimal Classification — is given for the majority of books.

The monthly issues of the *ANB* also lists government publications issued by the Commonwealth and the States. This service is further discussed in Chapter VI; here it will suffice to note that these entries for government publications are cumulated annually in *ANB*. In addition a separate annual volume issued under the old title *Australian government publications*[41] lists what is referred to in the introduction as "official publications of the Commonwealth of Australia, the Commonwealth Territories and the States". While the *ANB* includes in its entries "government publications both Commonwealth and State (including bills and acts of Parliament)", *AGP* excludes films, maps and single copies of acts and bills, the ordinances of the Territories, Arbitration Court awards, statutory rules and orders, and parliamentary notice papers, journals and votes and proceedings. This is a formidable list of exclusions which is difficult to understand when one takes into account the inclusion of issues of long established journals, e.g. "Australian science index: v. 7, no. 12 – v. 12, no. 11: Dec. 1963 – Nov. 1964, Melbourne" which is one of scores of similar entries in *AGP*. There appears to be no clear policy of selection of "official" or "government" publications (or both!) for inclusion in one annual cumulation rather than in another. Finally it must be noted that *ANB* includes pamphlets of five or more pages, maps, prints, sheet music, the first issue of each new periodical or newspaper and moving picture films produced in or relating to Australia.

Current bibliography is, of course, not limited to publications in monograph form. However, the bulk of references is such that it is impossible to issue a periodical list of them covering all aspects of a nation's life. Consequently these periodical indices are limited to one phase or another of Australia's cultural and intellectual life and it will be more appropriate to deal with them under the bibliography of the relevant subject. At this point it is important to note that P. H. Saunders of the National Library has edited a bibliography of periodicals, annuals and serials published in Australia, under the title *Current Australian Serials*.[30a] This select list first appeared in 1964 and a revised edition came out in 1966; it is based largely on the serials currently indexed in *Australian Public Affairs Information Service* and in *Australian Science Index*. Listings in *Current Australian Serials* are arranged under broad subjects, with bibliographic and purchasing details for each entry. There is also an index of titles and of organizations other than publishers who are responsible for serials cited.

The Australian book trade has developed over the years into a strong and successful section of the business world. Its specialist trade journal, *Ideas about books and bookselling*[98a] is published by the Melbourne firm of D. W. Thorpe Pty. Ltd. and contains every quarter a list of new Australian books. The quarterly list is cumulated every second year under the title *Australian books in print*.[36a] This is essentially a trade publication and does not lay any claim to being exhaustive; it is, however, fairly reliable for the output of commercial publishers in Australia and New Zealand. Though entries are compressed and do not meet a librarian's bibliographic standards, they do give the basic information necessary for procurement. In 1965 *Australian books in print* was incorporated in the same firm's *Booksellers' reference book*[151a] which also contains book trade information.

A particular aspect of national civilization – at once seminal and far reaching in all respects – is the intellectual work going on in the Australian universities, some of which is finding expression in research work reports and theses. Some aspects of this work are listed in subject bibliographies, many of which are published with varying regularity in specialist journals. However, a comprehensive list covering all university theses was prepared by M. J. Marshall in the form of a *Union list of higher degree theses in Australian university libraries,* 1959.[105] The *Union list* is classified and the base volume reports all theses accepted up to 1958. Irregularity in the administration of deposit regulations caused the omission of some older theses in the base volume, but the first and second *Supplements,* both issued in 1961, include most of the earlier omissions and also bring the *Union list* up to date. Supplements and eventual cumulations will provide for continuity of service. Of course, not all the work done in university departments leads to theses and the *Research reports,* now published annually by most Australian universities, provide a record of theses and, as well, of papers and books written by members of the staffs.

B. *Newspapers*

The intrinsic significance of Australia's daily press has always been recognized. The democratic temper of the country's politics has enabled the newspapers to reflect – albeit with varying degrees of accuracy – the daily life of the people. Many partisan statements have been made on the influence of the press in Australia but these are now more easily examined since two scholarly books have appeared on the subject. One, the result of a Fulbright student's enquiry, is W. S. Holden's *Australia goes to press,* 1961,[96] which contains a useful but not exhaustive bibliography (pp. 277-280); the work deals primarily with the organization of the press in Australia and its editorial practices. A companion study undertaken by an Australian scholar, H. Mayer, deals mainly with the press in its socio-economic setting. Mayer's

Current National Bibliographies and Indices to Newspapers

The press in Australia, 1964, contains extensive bibliographies which the author has fortunately issued separately as a processed handbook with the title *Bibliographical notes in "The press in Australia" and related subjects,* 1963[106a] The considerable volume of references — 76 foolscap pages, closely typed — does not by any means represent an exhaustive bibliography on the press in Australia and Mayer explains in his preface the limitations he has been forced to adopt. Nevertheless, the *Bibliographical notes* are a very important contribution to this subject and will remain the basis of further research.

Awareness of the need for press directories has existed for a long time and as early as 1882 there appeared *The Victorian press manual and advertisers' handbook.*[161a] The usefulness of such a directory is self-evident and even in retrospect this type of publication can be of help for the historian in search of data on defunct periodicals. The Country Press Ltd. (Sydney) has issued since 1914 sixteen editions of what is now called the *Media guide and press directory of Australia and New Zealand.*[106b] The latest edition (1964) provides State by State, details on the daily press, popular weekly and monthly magazines and certain annuals. Particular emphasis is laid on the advertising value of the publications cited, but this should not obscure the fact that press directories can often lead to information not easily obtainable elsewhere. Similar guides exist for each State of the Commonwealth sponsored usually by both the press associations and the advertising business.

Literary journals are in many respects — contents, make-up, objectives — quite different from the popular journal which is the main target of the advertising agency. J. Tregenza's *Australian little magazines, 1923-1954*[153a] discusses their significance, and his bibliography on pp. 88-101 offers a full description of each magazine together with an indication of where sets can be located. The survey does not include theatre magazines, anthologies, university and college magazines.

Two types of bibliographic guides have been developed to enable the student to find access to the more important newspapers of Australia. The Mitchell Library has probably the most comprehensive collection of Australian newspapers extant, and the *Bibliography of newspapers filed in the Mitchell Library and the general reference collection of the Public Library of New South Wales,*[7] compiled by J. F. Arnot in 1944, will always remain an important guide to the Australian press. As the demand for newspapers grew with the development of historical researches of all kinds, most of the large libraries tried to improve their holdings of this type of source material. Their holdings are recorded in the *Union list of newspapers in Australian libraries*[35] published in 1959 and 1960 by AACOBS and prepared by the National Library's Bibliographic Centre. This *Union list of newspapers* is divided into two distinct sections. The first deals with *Newspapers published outside Australia;* it appeared in 1959 and is arranged according to country of origin subdivided by place of publication. Supplements are being issued to bring the list up to date. Of greater interest to us in this context is the second section, *Newspapers published in Australia,* which first appeared in 1960. Entries are arranged by state and then by cities. A supplement containing amendments to 1960 was published in 1961. The significance of the *Union list of newspapers published in Australia* goes beyond the advantage of showing library holdings, because it provides a good deal of bibliographical history of many newspapers for which — in the absence of adequate historical accounts — there exist no other sources of information.

The only historical bibliography of Australian newspapers was compiled by J. Moore-Robinson and printed in *The Voice,* a Tasmanian socialist weekly, in 1933. It was reprinted as a pamphlet under the title *Chronological list of Tasmanian newspapers from 1810 to 1933.*[110] Though only a ten-page pamphlet, it gives a brief history of 109 newspapers — the date of their first and last appearances as far as could be established, as well as their changes of name and amalgamations.

A specialized union list of select newspapers was compiled as a by-product of the work of the Department of Demography at the Australian National University. This Department has for some time been engaged in an investigation of the process of migrant assimilation, and M. Gilson's *Bibliography of the migrant press in Australia, 1847-1962 (second draft)*[86] is designed as a bibliographic aid to the work of the Department of Demography, though it is, of course, also of great value to other students.

Though, strictly speaking, the index to a serial cannot be considered a bibliography proper, the indices to newspapers constitute a special case. The key organization of the press causes a large proportion of identical news to be released to many newspapers at the same time, though the reporting may occasionally

16

Current National Bibliographies and Indices to Newspapers
vary by a day from one paper to another. The index to any one
of the major newspapers is therefore a partial bibliographic guide
to all — the degree of coverage depending on the importance of
the news beyond any local scene. Only two of Australia's national
daily papers have issued a printed index. *The Argus index*[6] began
in 1910 and continued until 1949, covering almost one-third of
the life of this once famous paper which began in 1846 and ceased
publication in 1957. The other and perhaps more famous newspaper to issue an index, is the *Sydney Morning Herald*,[150]
founded in 1831, which has issued its index from 1927 to 1961;
during the years 1949 to 1953 it included references to the
Sydney Herald.

IV

BIBLIOGRAPHIES OF SUBJECT AREAS

The guides to published material on Australia mentioned so far are essentially universal in character. In consequence they are rather broad than deep, that is to say, they deal with the literature on Australia in a superficial and perhaps even haphazard way — haphazard in the sense that the exclusion and inclusion of items was often dependent on some accident of fate rather than on a scholarly plan. The bibliographies with which we shall deal in this chapter are distinguished by the fact that they were compiled to serve or illustrate a particular subject field or area of knowledge, such as history, literature, science.

However, there are some sources of reference which lump together a group of named and unnamed intellectual areas under the heading "Sociology" or "Social Sciences". The overlapping of interests and of contents, the looseness of terminology, the regrettably frequent vagueness of definition of the subject area itself, all contribute to a similar lack of precision in the respective bibliographies. It is therefore convenient to consider together as a group those which by consensus of opinion form part of the social sciences. The pure and applied sciences form another group easily distinguished as a large subject area in which the developments of this century have brought more overlapping and cross-fertilization than was thought possible before the end of the First World War. The third large group of subject bibliographies will contain literature and art. On investigation it will be realized that there are still large areas of virgin soil in the terra bibliographica Australiensis. If this study causes some of the virgin soil to be upturned it will not have been made in vain.

A. *The Social Sciences*

The Social Science Research Council of Australia — known from 1945 to 1952 as the "Committee on Research in the Social Sciences" — published between 1946 and 1954 eighteen issues of the *Australian social science abstracts*,[49] the first effort of this kind in Australia. Its publication was suspended because of want of finance and adequate staff, and the lack of demand. The *Abstracts* were replaced by surveys under the title *Bibliography of research in the social sciences in Australia;*[139] the first covered the years 1954-1957, the second 1957-1960. These surveys list work done in the universities, as well as research projects carried out by government departments or agencies, and show publications resulting from such research. Social sciences in the widest sense are also served by the important monthly index *Australian public affairs information service*.[46] Known briefly as APAIS, it has since 1945 been compiled by the National Library of Australia. Since 1955 the monthly issues have been cumulated into yearly volumes. APAIS is today the principal source of information for all periodical literature on the social sciences as well as on arts and letters in Australia. All entries are arranged under subject headings and from the 1964 cumulation on an author index has been added. This is a most welcome addition which will make the full exploitation of this important reference work much easier. A list of journals referred to and of "composite books and occasional literature indexed" is given at the beginning of each volume of APAIS. The books cited in APAIS represent a narrow and rather haphazard selection.

Similar ground is covered by the *Australian periodical index*[45] which appeared monthly between 1959 and 1964 as part of the *New South Wales Library Bulletin* published by the Public Library of New South Wales. The API has been partly cumulated in the *Index to periodicals*[117] produced by the Mitchell Library. This *Index to periodicals* has been maintained for many years and its first cumulation, covering the years 1944 to 1949, was issued in 1950; subsequent volumes cover the years 1949-1951, 1952-1955 and 1956-1959. The partial overlapping of the APAIS and the API is regrettable, but both indices have to be consulted by students wishing to obtain full coverage of Australian cultural and social conditions.

Since 1963 the Libraries Board of South Australia has tried to supply an indexing service to a restricted group of popular Australian periodicals which, it is claimed, are not indexed elsewhere. The index is called *Pinpointer*[122b] and covers in particular the interests of the non-academic engineer, the home mechanic, and the housewife. *Pinpointer* appears monthly and is cumulated annually, indexing 20 periodicals. While the coverage is interesting, it is a pity that we have here another fragmentary attempt which requires the efforts of expert staff without adding significantly to our bibliographic services. Some of the journals served by *Pinpointer* are indexed in APAIS and the inclusion of others raises serious questions regarding the principle of selection.

The Libraries Board of South Australia is also responsible for a new and promising venture in book review indexing. *The Index to Australian book reviews*98b is prepared by the Research Service of the Public Library of South Australia and appears quarterly, with an annual volume which cumulates material up to December. IABR includes reviews of books by Australian authors, of books published in Australia and books of Australian interest published overseas, and covers the journals indexed in *Pinpointer* as well as 28 literary and reviewing journals and newspapers.

(a) History and Geography

The history of Australia falls into four clearly distinguishable periods. There is first of all the very long period prior to the occupation of Australia by Great Britain; there is, then, the colonial period which came to an early end in the 1850's; thirdly, the period from the establishment of responsible self-government to the achievement of federation. The first half of the twentieth century would seem to form a suitable last period for the time being. Books dealing with Australian history may, of course, cover all or any combination of these periods. They may also be dealing with Australia as a whole or with the history of the separate states.

The first references to Australia occur naturally in the reports of voyages to and through the Pacific. Though the Terra Australis Incognita was not the prime goal for all who went either eastward from the Cape of Good Hope or westward from Cape Horn, it became, quite early in the great age of discoveries, an attraction for imaginative sailors of many nations. It also became — thanks to conflicting reports concerning size, climate, flora and fauna — the inspiration of several utopian accounts. In a period of European history as insecure and restless as the sixteenth and seventeenth centuries, the actual or imaginary search for a "terrestial paradise" had two peculiar results: while voyages in search of a better land were undertaken by publicly and privately sponsored explorers, the results of these expeditions were but rarely reported fully in print. Consequently, while the means to follow up discoveries appeared to be either lacking or were being withheld by those who financed them, the knowledge acquired was usually recorded in sealed letters and was not generally accessible. The mystery that surrounded Toscanelli's map and allegedly delayed the rediscovery of America was repeated many times in relation to the discovery of Australia.

Though not strictly speaking within the compass of Australian bibliography, it is worth noting that the earliest collective account of voyages to Australia was published in 1756 by Charles De Brosses as *Histoire des navigations aux terres australes.*[56] It is a collection of extracts from printed accounts of voyages to the Pacific in general and to Australia in particular, with a commentary in which the merits of each voyage are discussed and bibliographic references are given. Many of the accounts had been previously edited in collections of voyages, such as De Bry's, Hakluyt's and Purchas's, but there exists no earlier selection of extracts from voyages relating specifically to Australia and De Brosses can therefore be considered to have compiled the first annotated bibliography of this continent. His aim was to draw attention to the possible occupation and colonization of the continent by France. The English public, on the other hand, was stirred to think seriously of the advantages arising from the establishment of a colony on the immense southern continent by John Callander's *Terra australis incognita, or, voyages to the terra australis or southern hemisphere;* this appeared ten years after the work by De Brosses of which it is, to a large extent, a copy. Together with Alexander Dalrymple's *Historical collection of several voyages and discoveries in the south Pacific ocean,* published in London in two volumes in 1770-1771, these works formed the background of popular knowledge against which the voyages of Captain Cook stand out in the final act of discovery and description of the eastern coast of Australia. Of later collected editions of voyages to Australia, R. H. Major's *Early voyages to terra australis now called Australia,* 1859,[104] is worth mentioning. The editor was secretary to the Hakluyt Society but was attacked by some contemporary historians on account of his editorial work. A modern summing up is provided by J. C. Beaglehole in his *The exploration of the Pacific,* 1934,[50a] and still more recently in J. P. Faivre's *L'expansion française dans le Pacifique de 1800 à*

1842, 1953,[80] where French archival sources receive special attention.

The important Spanish voyages of discovery in the Pacific during the early 17th century have only recently received renewed attention. Australia is fortunate that the magnificent Dixson and Mitchell collections now in the Public Library of New South Wales, contained a very representative portion of Quiros material. The Trustees of the Library published in 1964 *A Catalogue of Memorials by Pedro Fernandez de Quiros*,[113b] which unfortunately deals with the Memorials only and does not refer to other Quiros material in the Library.

The most extensive guide to Spanish voyages published to date is Father Celsus Kelly's *Calendar of documents*: *Spanish voyages in the South Pacific*.[98c] Father Kelly, one of the foremost historians of Spanish-Pacific relations, provides not only an annotated chronological list of more than a thousand documents bearing on the voyages of Alvaro de Mendaña, Pedro Fernandez de Quiros, and the Franciscan missionary projects in the South Pacific, but also offers in his lengthy introduction basic general comment on the archival material and printed records to which his *Calendar* refers. An analytical list showing the distribution of documents in various libraries will save future historians the task of going on a lengthy pilgrimage in their search.

The voyages of Abel Janszoon in the 17th century and his mapping of the Australian coast received renewed attention when a collateral descendant of the great Dutch navigator visited Australia in 1963. To commemorate the occasion the Public Library of New South Wales issued a booklet under the title *Abel Janszoon Tasman: a bibliography*,[112b]. The items listed include related material in several libraries in Australia and abroad and since the bibliography shows locations, it is virtually a union list of material concerned with Abel Janszoon Tasman.

Cook's three voyages and the numerous works relating to them have received ample bibliographical treatment. The Mitchell Library issued in 1928 a commemorative *Bibliography of Captain James Cook*,[116] which lists the wealth of material in the Mitchell and other libraries; this is probably the most comprehensive bibliography even today. Sir Maurice Holmes prepared what he preferred to call *Captain James Cook, R.N., F.R.S., a bibliographical excursion, 1952*,[97] which replaced his earlier effort of 1936. Each entry is accompanied by a bibliographical description and notes. However, Holmes's bibliography is very limited, excluding "reprints, later editions, collected editions and abridgements"; it also omits most works in foreign languages where they are translations of English works or where they have not been translated into English. A more ambitious effort is S. A. Spence's *Captain James Cook, R.N. (1728-1779); a bibliography of his voyages, to which is [sic] added other works relating to his life, conduct and nautical achievements,* 1960.[143] Spence's bibliography is divided into works preceding the first voyage, works relating to each of the three voyages, collected editions, biography and miscellanea, and includes references in languages other than English. In the case of works not wholly concerned with Cook, a note indicates the pages where references to Cook can be found. Though the bibliography is somewhat amateurish, it is useful in the breadth of its coverage. Very nicely presented and suitably accompanied by a brief introduction and short notes is Rolf du Rietz's *Captain James Cook: A bibliography of literature printed in Sweden before 1819,*[71b] which lists 19 items related to Cook and his voyages; each entry has full bibliographic details and notes on variant editions.

Within a little more than a century after Cook's discoveries, colonists new and old had created a commonwealth on federal lines. The event, its preparation, achievement and aftermath, drew literary fire from scores of writers of all sorts: politicians, poets, demagogues and religious leaders — all made some contribution to the great welding process which culminated in the proclamation of the Commonwealth of Australia in 1901. A brief critical bibliography of the literature was compiled by Alan Gross under the title *Attainment*[93] and published by the "Bread and Cheese Club" of Melbourne, in 1948. The bibliography is very selective and the bulk of the entries are arranged according to location in various libraries.

The most significant bibliography of the history of Australia as a whole is contained in the *Cambridge history of the British Empire, v7 pt 1; Australia,* 1933.[60] It comprises no less than 72 pages and is divided into two major parts; the first deals with manuscript sources and official papers, described according to the holding library or collection, while the second lists "other works" and is arranged according to broad periods of history. The first section is today the more important by far, as it describes in some detail the relevant holdings of the Public Records Office, the

Admiralty, the Home Office, the War Office, the Exchequer and Audit Office, the Treasury, the Board of Trade, the Privy Council, and the Chancery. A footnote indicates the year up to which records are open to public inspection.* A select list of British Parliamentary Papers relating to Australia and, in a later section, a select list of Parliamentary Papers of the Australian States is also added. Of the manuscript sources the following are described briefly: the British Museum collections of the Sloane MSS, the Egerton MSS and the Liverpool MSS and "Varia"; the Church Missionary Society; the London Missionary Society; the Wesleyan Methodist Missionary Society; the Society for the Propagation of the Gospel; the Archives of the Australian states and the manuscript collection of the National Library of Australia, then known as the Commonwealth National Library, and of the Archives Nationales, Paris. The list of printed material contains a useful list of Australian newspapers and of such papers published in England which have special bearing on Australia. The last section of the bibliography, dealing with Cultural Development, is rather inadequate, but critical and bibliographical writing on this subject did not begin in earnest until the Second World War.

A short bibliography, significant for its special reference to archival collections, is appended to M. H. Ellis's *Lachlan Macquarie, his life, adventure and times,* 1947.[75] C. M. H. Clark's *A history of Australia,*[63] of which v1 appeared towards the end of 1962, also contains a bibliography judiciously entitled "A select bibliography" (v1: 389-410). Though it lists many works published after the Second World War, it necessarily repeats many of the entries of the *CHBE;* Clark's list also is divided into broad subject groups, though for the present these are limited to matters bearing on the early history of Australia to 1821.

There is no other bibliography of similar depth, but some useful select lists can be found as appendices to scholarly histories such as G. Greenwood's *Australia, a social and political history,* 1951,[90] where references published since 1928 are cited, and the annotated bibliography compiled by C. H. Grattan and published as "Bibliographical notes" at the end of his *The United States and the Southwest Pacific,* 1961.[89]

A brief annotated list of books on Australian history compiled by G. M. Blakeslee forms part of Section V of G. M. Dutcher's

---

* This date will now have to be brought forward since another 30 years have lapsed and more recent material will be accessible today.

Guide to historical literature, 1931,[72] which was sponsored by the American Historical Association. Blakeslee's list is rather inadequate and the new edition of the Association's *Guide,*[3] edited in 1961 under the chairmanship of G. F. Howe, contains a more up-to-date list — more comprehensive but less annotated — compiled by A. D. Osborn.

Some narrow aspects of Australian history have been covered by detailed bibliographical treatment as, for instance, the important question of land tenure and settlement by *The Torrens Australian digest,*[126] compiled by G. W. Power, Sir L. E. Groom and A. D. Graham, and by S. H. Roberts's *History of Australian land settlement,* 1924[129] (pp. 402-421). Another example of such useful small-scale bibliographies deals with Australia's *cause célèbre* of the 19th century, the Kelly Gang affair, which has been the subject of many official documents, historical and sociological essays and of innumerable pseudo-historical novels. A chronological list with annotations of the more important documents has been prepared by C. Turnbull as *Kellyana,* 1943.[154a]

Australian military history has attracted a good many writers, serious scholars as well as some whose imagination led them far into the realms of fiction. The only bibliography of non-fiction on Australia's military achievements was compiled by C. E. Dornbush, an American enthusiast who lists 544 titles in his *Australian military bibliography,* 1963.[71a] The work is divided into historical periods and the major armed conflicts in which Australians have taken part. Only a small selection of Federal and State Parliamentary papers on military matters are included and quite generally the bibliography is not claimed to be exhaustive. Many titles are annotated to show the content or character of the book and besides an author index there is a regimental index for both world wars as well as a list of "Official Publications" dealing with army orders and military forces lists.

Current work on the history of Australia is listed in the journal *Historical studies: Australia and New Zealand,*[95] which has appeared twice yearly since 1940.

The writing of Australian history has been hampered for decades by the absence of proper guides to the manuscript collection in our libraries and archives. Though many documents bearing on the 19th and early 20th century are still outside Australia and likely to remain so — albeit photographic copies are becoming more freely available — there are considerable collections of original diaries, note books, letters and the like in the State Libraries and the National Library of Australia. Many of these documents are of particular significance for regional studies and such guides as are available to State Archives are discussed in Chapter V below. Of interest to the broader view of Australian history is the *Guide to collections of manuscripts relating to Australia*[30b] which is being issued in loose-leaf form by the National Library since 1965. Its scope is adequately described in the introduction: "The purpose of this *Guide* is to direct research workers to manuscript source material relating to Australia and its Territories. It includes collections of Private Papers and Government Archives, or copies of them, wherever located". The *Guide* contains entries for archival units, arranged under group names, showing title, inclusive dates, quantity in terms of running feet, location, brief description, access conditions, and other essential information. A comprehensive index lists all personal and corporate names which occur in the *Guide,* whether these have appeared as authors, subjects, owners or in any other connection.

A descriptive list of maps relating to the early exploration of the Pacific can be found in R. A. Skelton's *Explorers' maps,* 1958.[134] Modern Australian cartography can be traced from 1946 onwards through the *Bibliographie cartographique internationale*[51] (where Australia is included in the section "Océanie"), as well as through the *Map catalogue*[20] of the National Mapping Office at Canberra and, since 1959, through the quarterly reports on *Maps received in the Mitchell Library*[118]. *The Australian geographer,*[39] which began in 1928, carries regularly a bibliography of Australian geographical literature, and the Institute of Australian Geographers lists since 1959 in its "service periodical" *Australian geographical record*[40] "A register of research in progress and a bibliography of publications". The most comprehensive retrospective bibliography of Australian maps published during the past two decades has been issued by the Department of National Development under the title *Index to Australian resources maps of 1940-59,* 1961.[18] The *Index* includes all maps showing economic and general resources with the exception of maps designed for junior school use and maps of very small areas, as well as maps which have become superseded by more recent editions; maps in foreign languages are also omitted. The entries are classified by broad subjects and cite, where applicable, single maps from atlases. Each subject group is geographically divided according to states, but all maps extending across state boundaries are included under "Australia". There is no index of compilers or titles or specific subjects.

Both the Australian Army and the Navy have not only contributed substantially to the mapping of Australia and the sea around it, but have also issued bibliographies of their maps and charts. The Army's Directorate of Military Survey published in 1962 a second edition of its *Catalogue of official military maps*[8] which shows the various series of maps issued or in preparation, together with a brief description of the geographical standards employed. The Department of the Navy published in 1962 a revised edition of its *Catalogue and index of Australian charts and Admiralty charts of Australian waters*,[24] which was prepared by the Hydrographic Service and is issued in loose-leaf form to allow for the addition of new pages. Information regarding new pages is advertised in the "Australian Notices to Mariners".

A major contribution to the bibliography of Australian geography has been made possible by recent developments in photo-offset-printing. The reproduction in book form of the American Geographical Society's *Research catalogue*[2]— one volume of which deals with Australia, New Zealand and the Pacific Islands — provides a unique list of references gathered in one of the world's greatest research libraries. The *Research catalogue* is arranged according to a special classification system devised in the Society's Library. Books and periodical articles are arranged in chronological order within each section, and users should carefully study the introductory pages if they wish to get the maximum use from the *Research catalogue*.

(b) Public Administration, Law, Politics

The area to be discussed here, "Public Administration, Law, Politics", is at once sufficiently defined and wide enough to bring together the bibliographies which exist in the Australian context without having to repeat the same sources of references under different chapters. However, one large single section has been purposely omitted: government publications. This exclusion is justified on the grounds that the form of publication of government papers, be they Australian or British, has brought with it particular types of reference — tools which are more easily treated separately. Nevertheless, it should be noted that some if not most of the bibliographies here cited include references to select government publications.

Whether politics — and consequently history — are "made" by individuals or by groups, there can be no doubt that the personal records of those who were involved in the government of a country form the source material on which historical writing and subsequent politico-social analysis are based. The archives of the Commonwealth and of the States contain private as well as public archives and guides to these holdings are important for any one interested in their use. Though the archival collections of the States are primarily concerned with regional and local history, it must be borne in mind that the Mitchell Library, Sydney, holds manuscript and archival material of singular importance for the whole of Australia. A special guide to a section of these manuscripts has been compiled by P. Loveday and H. Nelson in 1964 and published under the aegis of the University of Sydney's Department of Government and Public Administration under the title *Bibliography of selected manuscripts relating to Australian politics since 1890, held in the Mitchell Library, Sydney.* [99c] It is a descriptive list of manuscripts of political interest for the period from 1890 onwards, and is designed to be used as a supplement to archival lists which the Mitchell Library is preparing. In his introduction Loveday carefully explains the different manuscript collections he has worked on and the best use that can be made of his guide.

The process of government itself is the subject of Jean Craig's *Bibliography of public administration in Australia (1850-1947)*, 1955.[66] "The major part of the bibliography takes the form of a classification by subject of the relevant documents to be found in the papers of the New South Wales Parliament for the years 1856 to 1947 and of the Commonwealth of Australia Parliament for the years 1901 to 1947." This limitation is not evident from the title but users should be aware that little material from states other than New South Wales is cited. Nevertheless, Miss Craig's bibliography is the most extensive source of information on the literature of public administration in Australia.

As happens so often in a country organized politically on federal lines, the working of the constitution, its up-to-dateness and its ability to cope with changing economic conditions are constantly under review. The literature on the Australian constitution was first summarized by G. Greenwood in *The future of Australian federation,* 1946,[92] pp. 310-316. An interesting descriptive survey of the whole field of government and politics in Australia was published by L. Overacker in the "American political science review", September 1953, under the title *Publications on Australia useful to the political scientist: a selective survey.*[120] Overacker's bibliography is particularly useful on account of its detached evaluation of the material discussed.

A more recent list on *The literature of Australian government and politics,*[71] compiled by S. R. Davis and Colin A. Hughes, appeared in "The Australian journal of politics and history", 1958, in the form of a critical analysis of the temper and content of this literature. The same authors contributed a chapter to Livingston's *Federalism in the Commonwealth; a bibliographical commentary,* 1963.[99b] According to their own explanation, the bibliography on federalism includes many references listed in the 1958 survey but besides the necessary additions to cover the latest publications, they have also paid more attention to the specific aim of Livingston's book. L. F. Crisp added an extensive "Select Bibliography" to the 1965 edition of his standard work *Australian National Government* [66a] which had first appeared in 1949 under the title *The Parliamentary Government of the Commonwealth of Australia.* Crisp's list is very closely printed and contains several hundred references to books and periodical articles arranged under the chapter headings of the text of the book. A fourteen-page select bibliography of considerable merit accompanies O. M. Roe's *Quest for Authority in Eastern Australia, 1835 - 1851,* 1965.[129a] Roe's bibliography includes not only references to printed sources including 19th century Australian periodicals and newspapers but also to government papers, private archives and university theses.

A narrow aspect of constitutional thought is that concerned with the establishment of new states. The impetus of the New States Movement is largely centred on northern New South Wales and one of its most eloquent defenders is U. R. Ellis, who published in processed form *Australian new states movement: bibliography,*[76] in 1956. Ellis, who organizes the Office of Rural Research, Canberra (not a government agency), has also issued a *Bibliography [of the] Australian Country Party (Federal)*[77] and a similar bibliography for the New South Wales branch of the same party.[78] Slight though they are, a few roneoed foolscap pages each, they are the only separate bibliographies of any Australian political party.

Australia's relations with other countries have become a subject of academic study only during the last decade or two. The literature on foreign relations is consequently very slight. Relations between members of the British Commonwealth are, of course, a special aspect of these foreign relations, and P. E. Lewin's *A select list of recent publications contained in the Library of the Royal Colonial Institute illustrating the constitutional relations between the various parts of the British Empire*, 1926,[99] covers a period before, though leading up to, the Statute of Westminster which changed the constitutional structure of the British Commonwealth. Another bibliography bearing on Australia's foreign relations is the *Australian treaty list*[16] issued by the Department of External Affairs in 1956 with a supplement printed in 1962, which replaces the *List of international agreement (treaties, conventions, etc.) to which Australia is a party* . . . of 1935. The *Australian treaty list* includes all international agreements whether currently in force or not, including conventions, declarations, and exchange of notes, arranged into three sections: bilateral treaties, multilateral treaties and agreements with international organizations. Within each section entries are in chronological order, showing date and place of signature, brief description of content and references to the printed text. Two supplements have been issued to date, but the second includes all entries from the first in its cumulation.

While there are many law reports, there are few bibliographies of law in Australia. The basic reference work is Sweet & Maxwell's *Legal bibliography of the British Commonwealth of Nations*,[148] of which, in its second edition in 1958, v6 deals with Australia, New Zealand, and their dependencies up to 1958. The bibliography cites existing reports, digests, collections of statutes, etc.

An annotated list of judicial court decisions on a specialized aspect of public administration was compiled by R. J. Browning and A. R. Bluett under the title *A digest of Australian cases relating to local government reported up to the end of 1918*, 1919.[57] This important though now dated contribution to the legal bibliography of administration covers the decisions of all State courts and of the High Court of Australia as well as appeals to the Privy Council. Later decisions have to be traced through the digests of the various court reports.

A brief bibliography of Australian law is appended to *The Commonwealth of Australia, the development of its laws and constitution*, 1952,[121] which was edited by Sir George Paton within a series of books on the laws and constitutions of the British Commonwealth.

(c) *Economic and Social Conditions*

The writings on Australia's economic and social conditions, its finance, markets and trade are fairly numerous. Even early in the nineteenth century, tracts and books describing the economic life abounded to attract and sometimes to warn the prospective immigrant. There exists to date no separate bibliography of these books or pamphlets though they are, of course, included in such works as Ferguson's Bibliography or Foxcroft's Catalogue. With the twentieth century there came in Australia, as elsewhere, the specialist journal and the proliferation of professional economic writing. These, too, are still quite inadequately covered by bibliographies. The National Library issued in 1953 a processed list of titles *Select bibliography on economic and social conditions in Australia, 1918-1953*,[32] one of a series of specialized bibliographies. The National Library has issued scores of similar bibliographies, usually in response to specific enquiries or in anticipation of public and parliamentary interests. Though these lists are often short and quite narrow in contents, their total coverage is considerable. They are practically all run off on roneo stencils without any frills such as title pages, imprints, etc., but on account of their wide distribution in Australia they can well be considered as "printed sources of references".

A rather restricted but useful list of journal articles on Australian economics was compiled by Alicia Murdoch in 1964 under the title *Bibliography of selected periodical articles on Australian economic subjects, published in English outside Australia, 1946 - 1962*.[110a] It appeared in "The Economic Record" and contains 250 entries arranged under broad subjects and by date.

Some comprehensive bibliographies of specialized fields can be found as appendices to monographs, e.g., the very full survey of the literature on Australian currency and finance in S. J. Butlin's *Foundations of the Australian monetary system, 1788-*

1851, 1953,[58] pp. 555-573. However, Australia's long-standing interest in banking legislation has been the subject of the National Library's *Select bibliography: Australian series no 3*, which deals specifically with *Banking in Australia, 1911-1951*.[27]

Another useful bibliography on an important aspect of the Australian economy can be found in A. Barnard's *The Australian wool market, 1840-1900*, 1958,[50] pp. 207-214. A wide approach to marketing is covered by the *Select bibliography of publications on Australian agricultural marketing with comments on contents and character*[9] which was published by the Bureau of Agricultural Economics, Canberra, in 1957. Citation is limited to references that have bearing on "the movement of goods from the producer to the consumer, terminating where an agricultural product undergoes radical industrial conversion". The period covered is 1945 to 1957 with only one or two exceptions.

Since modern economics is completely dependent on statistical data, G. R. Palmer's *A guide to Australian economic statistics*, 1963,[120a] is a welcome aid to the location and interpretation of economic and sociological facts. Palmer's *Guide* includes "A survey of Australian statistical publications" (Chapter II) to which is added an appendix of 12 pages where these publications are listed in order of their source. The bibliographical detail is not satisfactory and it would have been well worth the trouble to indicate when the serials cited commenced publication. For further information on this topic, see the note on publications of the Bureau of Census and Statistics, p. 57 - 58.

It is somewhat surprising that so far very little has been done for the bibliography of Australian economic history. During the nineteenth century, hundreds of pamphlets were printed praising or condemning economic theories and practice. *A select bibliography of pamphlets on Australian economic and social history, 1830-1895*,[87] was produced by J. Ginswick in 1961. Ginswick's list, which is based on the holdings of the Mitchell Library, is arranged chronologically under subject divisions.

Labour relations and employment conditions are a basic part of the general social conditions of a country. In this field, too, the National Library has published a useful bibliography as part of its Australian series, *Conciliation and arbitration since 1947 [to April 1952]*, 1952,[30] with some brief annotations. The Industrial Relations Center of the University of Hawaii produced in 1961 a series of *Selected bibliographies on labor and industrial relations in Australia, India, Japan, New Zealand, Philippines.*[93a] The Australian section covers the years 1940 to 1960 and includes sources on the arbitration and conciliation system, but the list is altogether rather slight. Quite recently the Department of Labour and National Service issued a *Bibliography of official Commonwealth and state publications relating to labour matters,* 1962.[17] This booklet of 20 processed pages is intended as a general guide to publications in the field of industrial relations, and does not specify articles and books on the subject.

The recently established *Australian journal of social issues* contains in each issue *Abstracts from Australian material on social issues*[43] as well as more specialized bibliographies in this field. This type of current literature survey is, of course, very important and will, in a few years, provide a basis for comprehensive bibliographies. The journal "Labour history" which has been issued since 1962 by the Australian Society for the Study of Labour History, is also showing its awareness of the importance of bibliography as a basis for scholarly research. Besides several minor essays on the bibliography of labour, a really major contribution on industrial conditions and the development of labour legislation is E. C. Fry's *Parliamentary papers . . . 1856-1900 as a source of labour history,*[83a] which appeared serially between 1963 and 1966. This annotated bibliography deals with the parliamentary papers of each State from the beginning of self-government until the federation of the Australian colonies. Entries are grouped by subject and arranged in chronological order; the groups are numbered consecutively throughout the series of articles. Each entry is defined by its parliamentary session and the volume of the Parliamentary Papers in which it appears; the sessional number of each Paper is given except in the case of N.S.W. Papers.

An important social problem in Australia is the assimilation of migrants. W. D. Borrie, one of Australia's experts on population and demography, issued in 1953 a brief annotated bibliography on *The assimilation of immigrants in Australia and New Zealand.*[55a] The greater part of the work deals with Australia. Books and periodical articles are included, and there is also a separate list of unpublished university theses on the subject of migrant assimilation. The influence of foreign language newspapers published in Australia before 1939 and after 1945 is reflected in the separate list of these which fills four pages.

(d) Education

Among the many subjects related to sociology, such as education, philosophy, psychology and social psychology, only education is covered by a current bibliography, the *Australian education index*.[38] Issued since 1957 under the auspices of the Australian Council for Educational Research (ACER) it is not only the sole current bibliography in the field of Australian sociology but is also the only bibliographic effort based on library co-operation. The *Australian education index* contains entries from about 80 journals and also cites references to a considerable number of monographs on education and educational psychology. A separate section of the *Index* provides an information service for news items.

Special aspects of educational work are covered by two lists issued some years ago. The Department of Social Services issued in 1955 a *Select bibliography on child welfare*,[21] and the National Library issued in 1958 a bibliography under the title *Mentally handicapped children . . . a select list compiled in co-operation with the Handicapped Children's Association (A.C.T.)*.[31]

Two efforts have been made to establish a union list of educational periodicals in Australian libraries. *Education and related subjects: a list of periodicals in university, teachers' college and other education libraries in Australia*[149] was compiled by the Sydney Teachers' Colleges in 1951. In 1954 C. F. Dwyer, of the ACER Library, brought out a second edition of *Periodicals in education, psychology and related subjects in Melbourne libraries: a list*.[73]

ACER has also published a list of *Theses in education and educational psychology accepted for degrees in Australian universities, 1919-1950*, 1953,[37] and a supplement covering the years 1951-1953. The *Review of education in Australia*,[128] which has been issued intermittently by ACER since 1938, has carried some surveys of educational studies and research in progress, and a similar survey has been carried out since 1951 on an annual basis by the Commonwealth Office of Education under the title *Educational research being undertaken in Australia*.[11]

In a closely related field, the Department of Social Services issued a *Select bibliography on mental health*[23] in 1955; a *Select bibliography on juvenile delinquency*[22] was issued by the same agency in 1954.

Bibliographies of Subject Areas

During the past ten years there has been a considerable growth of public interest in the work and organization of Australia's universities and the consequent increase of published statements on the subject made N. Caiden's stock-taking useful and timely. Her *Bibliography for Australian universities*[59a] first appeared as a pilot survey in "Vestes", the journal of the Federation of Australian University Staff Associations. This first edition of the *Bibliography* is based on a projected sociological study which unfortunately was abandoned; as a consequence the bibliographical worry was also left incomplete. It was revised and brought up-to-date for E. L. Wheelwright's *Higher education in Australia*, 1965,[162a] in which it occupies 70 pages. Users should be aware, however, that the revised edition of this *Bibliography* is restricted and that all items prior to 1939 have been omitted (with two exceptions) as well as the sections of the original *Bibliography* which dealt with "official publications" of universities and with "student publications". Reference to both lists is therefore essential.

Harrison Bryan's pamphlet *Australian university libraries today and tomorrow*, 1965[57a] contains four and a half pages of bibliography on Australian university libraries and librarianship to mid-1965. All but two entries refer to writings published after 1935. Despite a few omissions, this is a useful piece of work on the heart of our universities. It should of course be noted that Bryan's bibliography is to a large extent also contained in Caiden's bibliography.

(e) Aborigines

Interest in the native population of Australia has always been great and from the beginning of European contacts they have been more often a subject of speculation than of investigation in the accounts of early voyagers. Serious study from an anthropological and sociological angle did not begin until the end of the nineteenth century, and the few major works on Australia's aborigines rarely contain extensive reviews of preceding investigations. A list of earlier bibliographies can be found in the works of Massola and of Greenway, both of which are further discussed below. These are now of little significance. Among several small-scale surveys, I. F. McLaren's *Victorian Parliamentary Papers relating to the Aborigines*[102b] is a useful lead to a

35

number of important statements from Government authorities. Printed books and articles on the Victorian Aborigines have been listed in Memoir No. 24 of the National Museum of Victoria as *Bibliography of printed literature upon Victorian Aborigines,* by A. Massola; [105a] this bibliography is arranged under localities and subject headings (both in one alphabetical sequence) with an author index. A bibliography covering a rather short period is A. R. Pilling's descriptive survey of post-war literature in *Aborigine culture history, a survey of publications 1954-1957.*[122a] He briefly describes the archæological work on the aborigines of each state as well as of writings on Australia as a whole and follows this up with a "Catalog of Publications" which is arranged chronologically under the names of authors. Though the survey is claimed to be limited to various writings published between 1954 and 1957, it also refers to many earlier standard works.

The most comprehensive and best organized bibliography on the Australian Aborigines is J. Greenway's *Bibliography of the Australian Aborigines and the native peoples of Torres Strait to 1959,* 1963.[89a] Greenway's work is of a high standard of competence and will be the foundation stone for all future work on the native tribes of Australia. Entries are arranged in alphabetical order of author and assigned a running number; a subject index preceded by a "Check list to indexed subjects" contains references not only to general categories but also to specific entries as, for instance, the names of mission stations, of tribes, etc. A list of periodicals referred to, covering 20 pages, completes this model bibliography.

The Australian Institute of Aboriginal Studies[42a] began in 1962 to issue half-yearly bibliographic surveys of the literature relevant to its interests. The first survey covered the period 1961 — September 1962; from then on each issue of about 12-16 pages covers periodicals and monographs that have appeared within the preceding six months. Entries are arranged under broad subject groups and there is to date no index to these bibliographies.

B. *The Pure and Applied Sciences*

Though Australia's early period of development coincides with the age in which the foundations of modern science were laid in Europe and in the USA, it is only natural that there was little time and money for research and creative work in this field in a country whose men were necessarily in the first instance concerned to survive in their struggle with the natural surroundings. Nevertheless, a good deal of work was done in the descriptive sciences even in the earliest days of British settlement. The strangeness of the fauna and flora impressed the early settlers, and some men with scientific backgrounds, soon began to make lists of the biological and geological phenomena around them. However, there are few bibliographic summaries to show these achievements, and most of them are distinctly amateurish in character. Nor is the dearth of monographs on the bibliography of Australian science relieved by adequate current bibliographic coverage, which did not begin until 1922 when the *Australian science abstracts*[47] began to appear. Sponsored and published by the Australian and New Zealand Association for the Advancement of Science, the *Abstracts* provided for almost 40 years a current survey of scientific work in Australia. Beginning with v17 (1938) they were issued as part of the *Australian journal of science* until they ceased in 1957. In that year the Commonwealth Scientific and Industrial Research Organization (CSIRO) began a new service which replaced the *Abstracts,* entitled the *Australian science index.*[48] Though its appearance on the Australian bibliographic horizon passed almost unnoticed at the time, it is today the most comprehensive source of reference to Australian scientific literature, and as a piece of bibliographic craftsmanship excels all other Australian periodical indices. Each monthly issue is paged separately, but the entries are numbered consecutively throughout the calendar year and are divided into broad subject fields with separate author and subject indices at the end of every issue. The December issue contains annual cumulations of both these indices; references are, of course, to the annual current number. The list of journals indexed is given in each issue under a somewhat deceptive introductory note called "Abbreviations used".

The relation between science and government has become the subject of much discussion during the past 20 years. The tremendous cost of scientific research on the one hand and the importance of such research for the economic development and possibly for the actual survival of a nation, make it inevitable that governments should put considerable sums at the disposal of agencies concerned with the organization of scientific research. The government's principal instrument concerned with the organization and co-ordination of such research is the Commonwealth Scientific and Industrial Research Organization. Established as early as 1926, it has excellent libraries in many parts of Australia and its Head Office Library is responsible for a good deal of bibliographic work. The publications by members of this very large organization are listed in the *Annual report*[12] submitted to the Commonwealth Parliament and printed as a paper of the House. It is worth noting that the *Annual Report* also includes a brief account of the various serials isued under the aegis of CSIRO (including references to changes of title and cessation of publication) and notes detailing technical reports prepared by the various divisions of CSIRO for Australian industry. However, the *Annual Report* does not contain a list of internal reports of the Organization nor does it list papers prepared for CSIRO conferences. In order to further the dissemination of scientific knowledge to all who may require it, the CSIRO began issuing a monthly list of papers and translations; though all entries have bearing on work done under the aegis of the CSIRO, not all of the papers cited are written by Australian authors or published in Australian journals. The index began in November 1952 under the title *Abstracts of published papers and list of translations;* this title was changed with v5 in 1957 to *CSIRO science index,* and in 1958 it was changed once more to become *CSIRO abstracts.*[59] Under this last title it is continuing today to provide a valuable service. It should be clearly understood that the *CSIRO abstracts* relate only to work in which the Organization is directly concerned. The efforts of the Head Office Library have lately been directed towards a cumulative index to the work of CSIRO staff and a pilot edition of *CSIRO published papers: Author index*[12a] is now complete. It includes references for all publications issued while an author was a member of CSIRO. A subject index to match the *Author index* is in active preparation.

(a) Botany, Forestry, Zoology

An early attempt to deal with *The bibliography of Australian economic botany*[103] was made by J. H. Maiden in 1892; however, only Part I was ever published.

The Division of Forest Products of the CSIRO issued a reliable *Bibliography on Australian timbers and other forest products*[13] in 1944, with three supplements to 1949; M. I. Hulme was the compiler. On the occasion of the FAO World Eucalypt Conference, held in Rome, 1956, the same division issued a *Bibliography on the utilization of the eucalypts*[15] which was also compiled by M. I. Hulme. This *Bibliography* is arranged according to the Oxford forestry classification and though it is very comprehensive, divisional reports are deliberately excluded; it was brought up to date on the occasion of the Second Eucalyptus Conference in Sao Paolo, Brazil, by a *Bibliography on eucalypts, 1956-61*,[14] also issued by the Division of Forest Products. Wider coverage is the aim of the *Bibliography on Australia's vegetation, forestry and timber resources*, published in 1948 as a supplementary volume of the *Bibliography on Australia for regional development purposes*[19] of the Department of National Development. Though this is a useful compilation, it is far from comprehensive and is biassed towards books and papers of significance to developmental projects.

The Forestry and Timber Bureau of the Department of National Development has issued *Annual Reports*[24a] since 1930 which like the *Annual Reports* of CSIRO, contain a list of publications by staff members of the Bureau. These lists are useful because they bring together the records of important investigations based on Australian research.

The high incidence of bushfires which year after year destroy portions of Australian timber resources and cause tremendous losses, has stimulated research into the effects of such fires by the Soil Conservation Authority of Victoria. A by-product of these investigations has been *An annotated bibliography of the effects of fire on Australian vegetation*,[157] by C. F. Cooper.

Of the varied and important fauna of Australia, only birds and insects have received reasonably adequate bibliographic treatment. G. M. Mathews issued in 1925 a *Bibliography of the birds of Australia*,[106] first as Supplements 4 and 5 of his famous survey *Birds of Australia, 1910-1927* (12 vols) but later reprinted as a separate work. Another full and more recent treatment of the literature on Australian birds was prepared by H. M. Whittell in 1954 as *A bibliography of Australian ornithology, 1618-1950*.[163] This is still a standard work and its usefulness is enhanced by biographical notes on collectors and writers. Australia's insects have been the subject of many papers and monographs; A. Musgrave compiled a *Bibliography of Australian entomology, 1775-1930*[112] in 1932, where he, too, included biographical notes on authors and collectors.

(b) *Geology and Mining*

The literature of Australian geology and related fields has been listed as early as 1881 by R. Etheridge and R. L. Jack in their *Catalogue of works, papers, reports and maps on the geology, palæontology, mineralogy, mining and metallurgy, etc., of the Australian continent and Tasmania.*[79] Though the work is dated, it is reliable for the period covered. The introductory sentence shows the keen perception of some scientists of the older school for the importance of bibliography: "The bibliography of geology and allied sciences has of late years reached such proportions that without aid derived from catalogues similar to the present, any attempt to master their literature would be futile."

To judge by the introduction to his *Bibliography of Australian mineralogy,*[4] the same spirit appears to have moved C. Anderson, whose work appeared in 1916. Anderson's *Bibliography* consists of author, subject and locality indices and includes all work on Australian mineralogy whether published in Australia or abroad. The broader aspects of Australian geological literature are covered by Sir T. W. E. David in his *The geology of the Commonwealth of Australia*[70] which was revised and supplemented by W. R. Browne in 1950. Bibliographies of regional geology have been published by the Departments of Mines of South Australia and of Victoria. The latter, *Biographical sketch of the founders of the Geological survey of Victoria. . .by E. J. Dunn, and bibliography by D. J. Mahony,* 1910,[156] is rather out of date and inadequate. However, E. N. Teesdale-Smith's *Bibliography of South Australian geology . . . up to . . . 1958,* 1959,[140] is a reliable work in which most entries are accompanied by a brief note, although the absence of a subject index is a serious defect. An extensive bibliography accompanies O. H. Woodward's *A review of the Broken Hill lead-silver-zinc industry,* 1965;[165] arranged in alphabetical order of authors it covers this highly important industry in all its aspects.

(c) *Mathematics*

Australian contributions to mathematics have been recorded by P. Sprent in *A research register of Australian mathematicians,* 1958.[144] The brief list of work published by living mathematicians — principally in Australian universities — was compiled for the

Australian Mathematical Society. Unfortunately, its title is misleading and the absence of a subject index renders the work almost useless. It is one of the many examples of misguided zeal which in the long run has prevented Australian bibliographical work from achieving reasonable standards of competence.

(d) Medicine

Medical research has been carried out for decades at the universities and teaching hospitals of Australia, but there exists no specifically Australian bibliography of publications related to this work. *The Medical journal of Australia* carries a series of *Abstracts from medical literature,* but these are not limited to Australian authors, nor are they necessarily concerned with specifically Australian subjects. An attempt to provide at least a guide to Australian medical writers was made by the Central Medical Library Organization, Melbourne, by issuing an *Author index to selected Australian medical periodicals.*[62] Only three issues have so far appeared, covering the years 1955 to 1957, and though the resources of the Centre have been inadequate to publish further indices since, preparations for the continuation of the *Author index* are in progress.

An interesting and perhaps surprising contribution to the bibliography of Australian science is B. Gandevia's *Annotated bibliography of the history of medicine in Australia,* 1955.[84] This is a work of high competence, the fruit of much medico-historical research, and based on a clearly conceived system. Gandevia's bibliography is arranged under seventeen subject groups; of these, the first four deal with the history of medical practice in Australia, one deals with specific diseases, one with aborigines, several with public health, etc. Each entry is separately numbered and to each section some spare numbers have been allocated for expansion. The *Index* includes references to authors, subjects, and also to the annotations which accompany most entries.

Another effort by B. Gandevia, this time assisted by A. Tovell, is aimed at providing a survey of "British views on Australian medical practice and . . . information on Australian medical problems published abroad". The compilers examined seven leading medical journals and extracted from them *References to Australia in British medical journals prior to 1880.*[153] The survey, containing 673 entries, was published in 1961 by the Medical Society of

Victoria. The entries are arranged according to the journal of origin and there is an author index as well as a subject list.

Those interested in the study of Australian mortality will be grateful for the exhaustive and thorough work of H. O. Lancaster which first appeared in "The Australian Journal of Statistics" with the title *Bibliography of vital statistics in Australia and New Zealand.*[98d] This list of over 1,500 references is arranged alphabetically by author and provided with an index according to diseases and another according to general subjects. The work is a by-product of a series of studies on mortality and was reprinted as a booklet in 1964.

(e) Agriculture

The meagre bibliography of the economic aspects of Australian agriculture has already been discussed on p. 25 as part of the bibliography of Australian economics, and the scientific aspects of the subject are, of course, fully covered by the indices and abstracts issued by the CSIRO.

Two bibliographies of Australian agriculture deal appropriately with the foundations of the country's economy, meat and wool. For the benefit of a specialist conference held in 1958, G. G. Allen produced *An Australian bibliography on original research on sheep and wool production with special reference to the Merino, 1946 - 1957*[15a] The bibliography was put together at the CSIRO sheep biology laboratory from references sent in by interested research workers and lays no claim to being exhaustive; unfortunately it is not very systematic either. Entries in part I are arranged alphabetically by author while those in part II — which appeared a year later — are divided into broad subject areas and then arranged alphabetically. It should also be noted that the title of part II has been changed by omitting the reference to original research and to the Merino. The continuations promised in the introductions to both parts have never been published.

A more competent piece of work is A. G. Culey's *Bibliography of beef production in Australia (c. 1930-1958)*[68] which appeared in 1961 and deals with all facets of the beef industry from breeding to transport; entries are chronologically arranged under topics, and there is a useful publications index besides author and subject indices. The publications index shows the periodicals searched, the volume coverage and references to entries in the bibliography.

Mainly, but not solely, concerned with agriculture in Australia is L. Davey's excellent *CSIRO water research bibliography, 1923 - 1963.*[69] The work lists the contributions CSIRO has made to water research during 40 years. The references are arranged chronologically under subjects, with excellent cross references from various headings, and an author index.

(f) Aviation

It is not surprising that the distances between population centres in Australia should have been a stimulus to transport economists and aviation experts. Though there exists no survey of the literature of transport in general, I. F. McLaren has compiled a very useful review of air transport in Australia in his *Australian aviation, a bibliographical survey.*[102] First published in the Victorian historical magazine and re-issued as a pamphlet in 1958 the *Survey* contains a discussion of aviation literature in Australia and a bibliography which is notable for its clear setting and accuracy.

(g) Meteorology

Though polite society supposedly no longer permits discussion of the weather as an opening gambit for the stranger in the drawing room, Australia's dependence on climatic conditions and the natural interest in civil aviation have greatly promoted the scientific study of weather conditions. The Bureau of Meteorology is responsible for a good deal of this research and publishes a number of series containing reports and data. In 1960 the Bureau issued a *List of Publications, 1945-1960*[9a] which, bringing earlier lists up-to-date, provides an index to reports, etc., published after 1945, and some observation reports of earlier date. Entries are arranged according to the series or journal where the article was published; there is, unfortunately, no index.

C. Literature, Fine Arts, Religion

(a) Literature

Australian literature — by which term we mean Australian letters, belletristic and poetry — has been fortunate in having attracted professional bibliographers at a fairly early date. Sir John Quick,

43

one-time Postmaster-General, issued a preliminary survey of Australian literature under the title *A classified catalogue of books and writings by Australian authors*, 1927.[127] His more extensive collection of data remained unsorted until E. Morris Miller took it over, sifted it, added to it and formed it into what has become one of the landmarks of Australian bibliography: *Australian literature from its beginning to 1935: a descriptive and bibliographic survey of books by Australian authors in poetry, drama, fiction, criticism and anthology with subsidiary entries to 1938*, 1940 (2 vols).[108] The work deals with the whole of Australian literature and literary criticism, arranged according to literary form. The large section on poetry is further divided by states. The importance of this great work lies in its critical evaluation of writers and their works, which precedes the chronological bibliography of the three basic literary forms: poetry, drama, prose fiction. The assessment and bibliography of Australian literary criticism includes writings by Australians on all literatures, English and foreign. There are three indices, a subject index to fiction, an index of subjects and name-subjects, and a general index of Australian authors including pseudonyms and anonyms. An alphabetical list of non-Australian authors of novels associated with Australia is also added. A work of this magnitude cannot but have some lacunae; its critical section, too, cannot be considered the final judgment for all times. But it is the product of the first serious stocktaking, it does not neglect the lesser figures and its bibliographic details are such that no one working on Australian literature can do without Miller's work.

Alas, *Australian literature from its beginning to 1935* has been out of print for many years. However, in 1956 there appeared a so-called "revised and extended edition", edited by F. T. Macartney under the title *Australian literature; a bibliography to 1938 by E. Morris Miller, extended to 1950, ed. with a historical outline and descriptive commentaries*.[109] The work is in truth not a revised edition of Miller's bibliography at all. It is an entirely new compilation based, indeed, on Miller's labours and incorporating the greater part of his bibliographical information, but omitting his connecting discourses and his extensive commentaries. Miller's quasi-lectures on various aspects and periods of Australian literature have been completely done away with, and the bulk of the original two volumes reduced to one single volume. Macartney's *Australian literature* is arranged strictly alphabetically, thereby avoiding the need for the three indices of Miller's work, and there is, of course, much advantage in such an arrangement. Some 300-odd authors have been given commentaries relating to their writing and stature but these commentaries are factual and not intended to be critical evaluations. The importance of Macartney's bibliography lies in its conciseness and in its coverage of the period from 1940-1950, which saw a great resurgence of Australian creative writing.

The only noteworthy effort in Australian literary bibliography prior to Morris Miller was P. Serle's *A bibliography of Australasian poetry and verse, Australia and New Zealand*,[133] which appeared in 1925. This scholarly piece of work lists in alphabetical order all Australian and New Zealand poets who have any serious literary merit. An appendix contains a list of those volumes of verse which would form a basis for a significant collection of Australian poetry.

During the past decade the bibliography of Australian literature has received considerable detailed attention. W. Stone edits an excellent series *Studies in Australian bibliography, 1954-*,[147] which so far contains reliable surveys of the literary output of J. Furphy, C. J. Brennan, R. Bridges, T. A. Browne (Boldrewood), H. Lawson; some of these were compiled by Stone himself. Stone has also collaborated with G. Mackaness in an annotated bibliography *The books of The Bulletin 1880-1952*, 1955.[101] In addition, since 1947 he has been editing the journal *Biblionews*[52] for the Bookcollectors Society of Australia; this journal, though cheaply duplicated, contains numerous bibliographic contributions of significance. Stone's bibliographic work is already having its influence on the academic approach to Australian literary studies.

A useful addition to the bibliography of Australian poetry — though rather a finding list than a bibliography — is E. I. Cuthbert's *Index of Australian and New Zealand poetry*,[68b] which was published in New York, in 1963. This is the kind of index much beloved by reference librarians who are frequently harassed by cross-word puzzlers. The *Index* is not, as one might be led to believe by the title, a bibliography of all poetry published by Australians and New Zealanders, nor is there an introduction or a preface to warn the user that this *Index* is merely an index to 22 collections (including some annuals such as "Australian Poetry") of verse published between 1888 and 1960. Nor is there any indication whether the 22 collections indexed are the most important ones, or the only ones, or why they were chosen in the first place. The *Index* contains lists of authors, of titles and of first lines; references from titles and first lines lead back to the author list which is the main index. In the case of voluminous authors whose longer poems may be divided by sub-titles, one can find the note "see forward . . ." or "see back . . .", expressions to which some of us are not yet accustomed.

H. Anderson, who contributed frequently to Stone's bibliographic enterprises, issued in 1953 an interesting *Guide to ten Australian poets*,[5] in which he cites in chronological order the work of what are, in his opinion, the ten most important Australian poets, together with a bibliography of significant critical writing about them. Bibliographies of the greater and popular poets are also beginning to appear, e.g., Mackaness's *Annotated bibliography of Henry Lawson*, 1951,[100] and I. F. McLaren's study of *C. J. Dennis, his life and work*, 1961.[102a] The growing awareness of the need for sound bibliographic foundations among the historians and critics of Australian literature is having its effect upon scholarship of this type.

An interesting excursion into a specialist field of prose writing is Graham Stone's *Australian science fiction index, 1939-1962*.[145a] This *Index* covers, according to the introduction, all the science fiction published in Australia either in magazines or in paper-covered book form; this last qualification for inclusion must be carefully remembered if one examines the *Index* critically. However, the compiler claims to have been generous in his interpretation of the term "science fiction". The *Index* consists of a contents analysis of seven magazines and five series, an author and a title list. Two pages of terse notes complete this useful but poorly produced bibliography.

There is still much scope for the regional treatment of Australian literature and J. H. Hornibrook's *Bibliography of Queensland verse with biographical notes*, 1953,[98] is an example of a move in that direction. Hornibrook chose two years' residence as a qualifying criterion for his *Bibliography of Queensland verse*, in which authors are arranged alphabetically with a short biographical sketch after each name.

The significance of the literary magazine as a factor in the formation of literary trends is discussed by Tregenza in his *Australian little magazines*[153a] which has already been mentioned on p. 15.

Bibliographies of Subject Areas

An endeavour to list current research on Australian literature can be found in the Tasmanian journal *Australian literary studies*[43a] – whose June issues for 1964 and 1965 contain an "Annual bibliography of studies in Australian literature". These bibliographies are divided into two parts: a general section listing surveys and criticisms of Australian history, and another section listing studies of individual Australian writers.

(b) Fine Arts

The only significant bibliographies on art in Australia – or more precisely, of works dealing with Australian art – are contained in three works by Bernard Smith. In his *Place, taste and tradition*, 1945,[138] in his *European vision and the South Pacific, 1768-1850*, 1960[137] (which, as the title indicates, is more concerned with the impression Australia made on the European mind), and in his *Australian painting, 1788-1960*, 1962,[136] Smith has provided bibliographic appendices which are fairly comprehensive.

(c) Religion

Though various Christian denominations took an early interest in Australia, either with a view to establishing missions to convert the Australian native population, or to catering for the felons and convicts who were certainly in need of faith, hope and charity, there exists only one bibliography of religion in Australia: R. Streit's *Missionsliteratur von Australien und Ozeanien, 1525-1950*,[146] issued in 1955 as v21 of the publications of the Roman Catholic "Institut für missionswissenschaftliche Forschung". The bibliography contains 1,410 entries, arranged chronologically and provided with a great deal of descriptive detail, contents lists where applicable, and notes concerning authors. As an example of bibliographic scholarship it is quite outstanding.

V

REGIONAL BIBLIOGRAPHY

It is impossible — and indeed it would be quite illogical — to try to separate a bibliographic survey of a country from its natural and historical development. The political development of Australia has been uneven in speed and depth, and its effect upon Australian bibliography is quite naturally equally uneven. To this historical background we must add the tremendous effect of Australia's geography: size of area and uneven spread of population. One conditions the other, but this is not the place to discuss the primacy of one cause or another. There is not one aspect of culture and civilization in Australia which has remained unaffected by the three factors: size of the continent — spread of population — uneven politico-economical development. The bibliography of Australia quite naturally reflects these dominant chords and nowhere as clearly as in the literature of the separate regions of the Commonwealth.

Mention has already been made of the *Classified and selective bibliography on Australia for regional planning purposes,* 1948-1950,[19] which was issued by the Regional Planning Division of the Department of National Development (known from 1943-1949 as the Department of Post-War Reconstruction). This *Classified and selective bibliography* covers in so many separate volumes New South Wales, Victoria, South Australia and Western Australia, as well as the Northern Territory. These bibliographies were intended principally to serve the Department's needs for the economic development of Australia, and the selection of entries was understandably biased towards references dealing with the industrial, agricultural and mineral potential of each region. Nevertheless these planning bibliographies are important milestones in the field of regional bibliographic surveys and it is regrettable that the sections on Queensland and Tasmania have so far not been published. Queensland in particular has, until now, been very poorly served by bibliographers. Nor is New South Wales, the oldest of the Australian States, very well

48

covered by bibliographies. The Public Library of New South Wales issued a list of *Works on New South Wales, compiled ... under the direction of R. C. Walker*,[114] in 1878, but this has, of course, been long out of date. Recently, however, a part of New South Wales has been well served by a useful literature survey. The *Bibliography of the Hunter Valley Region, N.S.W.*[63a] compiled by W. G. Coffey for the Hunter Valley Research Foundation, is a list of books and articles, broadly classified, for an area of New South Wales which is of great economic importance. Coffey's work, though stated to be selective, covers the field with care; the high standard of bibliographic form makes it a pleasure to use this publication.

Since 1959 the Archives Authority of New South Wales* has begun issuing preliminary inventories of some of its important documents; the first to be so treated were the *Records of the Colonial Secretary of New South Wales*.[115] In 1965 the Archives Authority prepared further assistance to scholars in need of a comprehensive guide through the wealth of its primary sources through the publication of a *List of series titles in the Archives Office of New South Wales*.[112a] It is emphasized in the introduction that this list is preliminary and additions and corrections will be issued at some future date, possibly in loose-leaf form. Reference to Loveday's *Bibliography of selected manuscripts relating to Australian politics*[99c] has already been made in Chapter IV, section A (b), but students should be aware of the fact that it is closely linked with the inventories mentioned in this paragraph.

In 1884, J. B. Walker compiled a *List of books relating to Tasmania* which was reprinted in 1899 in the Union Steamship Co.'s *Tourists' guide to Tasmania*[162] with the slightly altered title *List of works relating to Tasmania*. This list has only recently been superseded by E. D. Flinn's *The history, politics and economy of Tasmania in the literature, 1856-1959*, 1961,[82] a reliable and very useful guide to Australia's second oldest state. The initial date is, of course, that of the establishment of responsible government in the state. Flinn's bibliography is arranged under subject headings and includes the few specialized lists of references published in the past.

The Tasmanian State Archives published as processed docu-

---

* "The Archives Office of N.S.W." established in June 1961 as the administrative organ of the "Archives Authority of N.S.W." supersedes the "Archives Department of the Public Library of N.S.W."

ments two indices to archival materials relating to Tasmania. These inventories of record-groups were begun in 1957, covering six government departments. Of the projected detailed series *Guide to the public records of Tasmania*,[151] three sections dealing with the record groups of the Colonial Secretary's Office, the Governor's Office and the Convict Department have so far been issued.

Victoria was fortunate in attracting special attention from the bibliographer E. A. Petherick, whose *Bibliography of the State of Victoria, historical, descriptive, statistical*[122] appeared in several issues of the *Victorian historical magazine* for 1911-1913. This *Bibliography* is by no means easy to use; it is arranged loosely by subject, i.e., various important events in the history of Victoria and descriptions of the country are treated chronologically, with substantial portions from some reference quoted and numerous descriptive books and some journals extensively analyzed. There is no index. At the end of the first instalment (v2:47-48, 1911) Petherick added an explanatory note in which he announces that the "tentative form" of this work is "but a specimen of a Bibliography of Australasia and Polynesia, which would occupy 2,000 octavo pages". He then explains the arrangement of the whole work and makes it clear that the *Bibliography of the State of Victoria* is only a small subsection of the regional division. The fate of Petherick's own collection has already been mentioned at the beginning. Ill-health prevented him from putting his great bibliography into publishable form and the Victorian section is a rather unattractive sample.

The History Department of the University of Melbourne began in 1949 to prepare an annotated guide to Victorian historical source materials and a preliminary inventory was issued as Part I of the *Victorian historical documents*.[107] This is in effect a summary index to documents in the State Library of Victoria, to official sources and Victorian newspapers in the same Library and to selected theses in the Library of the University of Melbourne. A more comprehensive list of Victorian archival material in the State Library was published in 1961 with the title *Catalogue of the manuscripts, letters, documents, etc., in the private collection of the State Library of Victoria*.[160]

A *Bibliography of South Australia*[85] was compiled by Thomas Gill as early as 1885. This was a fairly substantial effort, with entries arranged under broad subject headings, and separate sections dealing with pamphlets, newspapers, government publications and maps. Though a few South Australian bibliographies can be found as appendices to books dealing with one aspect or another of the history of the state — e.g., Threadgill's *South Australian land exploration, 1856 to 1880,* 1922[152] — there has been no comprehensive bibliography issued since Gill's work of 1885. However, in 1962 the Libraries Board of South Australia began the publication of a journal *South Australiana*[141] which features a list of historical records received in the Archives Department of the Public Library as well as a list of publications printed in or relating to South Australia and in that Library.

Gill also compiled a *Bibliography of the Northern Territory*[85a] which during most of his lifetime had been under the administration of the government of South Australia. Gill's list, originally published in 1903, unavoidably includes many items already listed in his *Bibliography of South Australia* and the arrangement of entries is the same as in his earlier work. C. H. Hannaford prepared two supplements to the *Bibliography of the Northern Territory* containing entries up to 1938, which are included in the xerographic reprint of the original work issued by the Public Library of South Australia in 1962. Since the Second World War, the Commonwealth Government has taken a more active interest in the Northern Territory and other areas off the Australian mainland. The small volume of publications that has emanated from Government Departments in this connection, is described in an *Annotated bibliography of select government publications on Australian territories, 1951-1964.*[23a] It is divided into two parts, one general section which contains entries under author and subject, and another arranged according to the administrative divisions of the Ministry for Territories. The cross references from one section to the other are not always quite clear but this is a useful guide to public and semi-public statements on areas of increasing importance to Australia.

Western Australia — Australia's western third — has comparatively recently been treated bibliographically in F. G. Steere's *Bibliography of books, articles and pamphlets dealing with Western Australia issued since its discovery in 1616*[145] which appeared in 1923. A very substantial and comprehensive index to its sources has been started by F. K. Crowley, *The records of Western Australia,*[67] of which only one volume has so far appeared — in 1953.

Though Australian regionalism has for the most been confined within the boundaries of each state, the necessity of developing natural resources wherever they be found and the exigencies of hydrotechnology have forced upon reluctant parochialists several development schemes which exceed the historic limits of state regions. The Department of National Development again paved the way, and its Murray Valley Resources Survey Committee submitted a *Report . . . on resources and development of the Murray Valley,* in 1947,[111] which contains an extensive bibliography of the Murray region in the first volume.

A good example of a bibliography of a small region is provided in the centenary history of Queensland's capital: *Brisbane 1859-1959, a history of local government.*[91] This lavishly produced book, edited by G. Greenwood, has a seven-page appendix listing primary and secondary sources for the city's history.

The spate of histories celebrating the centenary or similar anniversaries of towns of all sizes, are rarely accompanied by bibliographies of any significance, but A. Coulls, City Librarian of the City of Broken Hill, has brought out a fourth edition of a concise *Bibliography of books, pamphlets, maps, etc., on Broken Hill and district,* 1965,[65] which may well serve as an example to other municipalities and districts anxious to record their history.

VI

GOVERNMENT PUBLICATIONS

Several references have already been made in earlier sections to various aspects of Australian life and civilization which are dealt with in "official publications". "Official publications"— the inverted commas will be dispensed with from now on — are documents emanating from government agencies and relating to administrative activities of such agencies in relation to the Australian scene. While the political history of the country is quite naturally reflected in the changing authorship of such official publications, it must be equally obvious that the social and economic history of Australia, from the beginning of British rule through the struggles for independence and right up to the very present, is contained in the official papers of British and Australian governments. In particular, it must be borne in mind that almost two-thirds of Australia's British history falls into a century in which governmental activities invaded on an ever-increasing scale the private domain of the citizen, and the justification and explanation of such activities became more and more important if elected governments were to retain their popularity. Indeed, Austin Smyth, one-time librarian to the House of Commons, wrote at the beginning of this century: "A popular government can hardly be conducted without an abundance of published information".*

British administration of Australia was, of course, principally in the hands of the Secretary of State for the Colonies and most of the files of that office are held in the Public Records Office, London. A number of bibliographies and calendars provide a guide to the materials of Australian interest in the Public Records Office. The Australian volume of the *Cambridge History of the British*

---

* Adam, M. I., and others. *Guide to the principal parliamentary papers relating to the Dominions, 1812-1911,* 1913 — The preface consists mainly of some excellent notes on the origin and history of Parliamentary papers by A. Smyth.

Empire[60] offers at the beginning a description of the Colonial Office and Public Records Office files; another brief description of colonial papers in the Public Records Office can be found in the second volume of Giuseppi's *Guide to the manuscripts preserved in the Public Records Office,* 1923-24.[88] However, none of the existing printed indices offer anything like adequate guidance to the research student.

Besides the Colonial Office despatches, letters and reports, there have also been discussions of Australian affairs in the British Parliament. The indices to the British Parliamentary Papers are therefore a significant source of information, especially those covering the end of the eighteenth and the first half of the nineteenth century. Besides the general indices to the House of Commons papers and journals, there exist some useful selective lists in which the more important papers and reports are cited. Most important among these is the *Guide to the principal parliamentary papers relating to the Dominions, 1812-1911,*[1] compiled in 1913 by M. I. Adam and others. Arranged according to Dominions, the Australian section occupies pp. 37 - 65.

The establishment of responsible government in the eastern states in 1856 and 1859 brought with it the establishment of parliaments and consequently the publication of legislative documents. Today, Australia is blessed with seven Parliaments and great opportunities to apply social ideals to the practical national way of life. The parliamentary papers of the State Parliaments are therefore quite naturally full of important statements concerning the economic and political conditions of the country. Smyth's assessment of the importance of public statements by parliamentary governments seems to have been heeded particularly well by Australia's political leaders. The indices to these parliamentary papers represent the only general key to this whole group of publications. Consolidated indices covering various periods exist for each group of parliamentary papers, but the standard of indexing leaves much to be desired. Not only is there no uniformity of terminology but there is also little consistency of usage within each set of indices. The most serious problem connected with the use of these indices lies with the indiscriminate use of catchword titles as order media.

The foundation of the Commonwealth of Australia brought with it the establishment of the Commonwealth Parliament and of Federal Ministries, bureaux and offices, all of which seem to be imbued by the principle: publish or perish. The papers of the Commonwealth Parliament are indexed very much on the standard of those of the State Parliaments, but a cumulated index was published in 1955 under the title *First consolidated index to the papers presented to Parliament, 1901-1949*.[36] This consolidation covers the first to the eighteenth Parliaments. There are also, of course, indices to each completed set of volumes of these papers. The criticism already made with regard to the indices of state parliamentary papers applies to some degree also to the indices of the Commonwealth papers.

There have been several attempts to bring the huge volume of government publications — i.e., of publications issued by the executive and administrative offices of the Crown — under bibliographic control. Noteworthy and already mentioned earlier is A. B. Foxcroft's *Australian catalogue*, 1911,[83] which includes all government publications in print at that time. These publications are divided into two groups: those emanating from the Government Printing Offices of New South Wales, South Australia and Victoria are listed in a special appendix, while those coming from similar offices in Queensland, Tasmania and Western Australia are incorporated in the main body of the catalogue.

A useful descriptive survey of Australian government publications was issued by the Joint Library Committee of the Parliament of New South Wales in 1965 under the title *Government documents in Australia*.[119a] It consists of a dozen articles by various authors on the structure and characteristics of government documents with particular reference to parliamentary papers. Besides some general comments, there are also more detailed treatments of the government documents of New South Wales, Queensland, South Australia and Tasmania. It is unfortunate that there are no contributions dealing with Victoria, Western Australia and the Commonwealth. Especially designed for the use of librarians and the general reader careful study of this survey is essential for all newcomers to the complex field of official publications of State Governments in Australia.

Attempts to index Australian government publications were not made again until the National Library began issuing its *Annual catalogue of Australian publications*,[25] which has already been discussed in detail in Chapter III. Suffice it here to point out that the *Annual catalogue* included a list of Commonwealth and State publications in the issues for 1937 (no. 2) to 1940 (no. 5) and again in the issues for 1945 (no. 10) to 1960 (no. 25), the gap in recording being due to wartime regulations. A monthly bulletin wholly dedicated to government publications appeared from 1952 to 1960 under the title *Australian government publications.*[42] The entries from these monthly bulletins were cumulated in the *Annual catalogue* mentioned above. As from 1962 and covering the year 1961 an *annual* index with the same title, *Australian government publications,*[41] is providing a guide to this vast group of serials, series and monographs. Though *Australian government publications* duplicates to some extent entries already listed in the monthly issues of the *Australian national bibliography,* it does not include single copies of acts, bills, ordinances, or statutory rules (all of which *are* shown in the *Australian national bibliography*).

In October 1965 the Commonwealth Government Printing Office finally began the publication of its own regular list of official documents issued under its imprint. *Commonwealth publications*[64a] appears monthly and is consolidated at irregular intervals; it replaces therefore with respect to the publications of the Commonwealth authorities, the monthly survey *Australian government publications* mentioned in the preceding paragraph. (The confusion of synonyms is barely relieved by the new list and neither users nor students will be happy with the inadequate coverage of current official documents which in effect persists.) *Commonwealth publications* list Parliamentary Papers — the first consolidated issue contains a list of all Parliamentary Papers for the sessions 1960/61 to 1964/65 — Acts, Statutory Rules and departmental papers and serial publications that fall within the jurisdiction of the Publications Department of the Commonwealth Government Printing Office.

An interesting contribution to the bibliography of Commonwealth government publications is the *Checklist of serial publications of the Commonwealth of Australia,* 1962.[29] This checklist has been issued by the National Library as a by-product of its *Union catalogue of periodicals in the social sciences and humanities* which as *Serials in Australian libraries* is mentioned in Chapter VII on bibliographical enterprise in Australia. The *Checklist of serial publications of the Commonwealth of Australia* is limited to the official publications of the Federal Government and Federal agencies. This *Checklist* was issued in 1962 and should be considered as a "pilot list"; though it shows library holdings as reported at date of publication, a careful search found this information quite unreliable. Current and non-current serials are listed in an alphabetical sequence in which the words "Bureau of" and "Department of" have been placed behind the critical name of the government agency's title.

Because the *Checklist* is a mere photographic copy of the Union Catalogue maintained by the National Library the word "Australia" which is, of course, part of the corporate author entry, has been retained. This has some effect on references from entries under the word "Australia" to entries beginning with the word "Australian" as the latter are not included. One can, of course, deduce — and rightly — that the entry referred to does not represent a government publication even if a government agency is connected with its production.

The strange variety of subjects with which governments and their publications are concerned has quite naturally some bearing upon the provision of bibliographic guides. Few departments have so far made any real attempts to trace the volume of their own literary production, with the notable exception of two of them.

Of the many administrative divisions of the Federal Government responsible for the publication of information, there are two whose output far exceeds that of all other divisions put together: they are the Commonwealth Bureau of Census and Statistics, and the Commonwealth Scientific and Industrial Research Organization. The *Annual report*[12] of the latter, issued since 1926-27 as a parliamentary paper — but recently printed in a handy format instead of in the large and unwieldy folio size — contains a list of publications issued by the organization, and since the 1944-45 Report, publications by officers of CSIRO are also included. The important bibliographic work done by CSIRO has already been discussed in detail in the survey of guides to Australian scientific literature, and the reader is referred to that section for information.

The publications of the Bureau of Census and Statistics are second to none in importance for all who want to have key information concerning Australia's social and economic life. The Bureau issues an annual list[10] of its publications arranged in two main sections, one relating to publications of the Central Office, further subdivided under subjects and frequency of appearance, and another relating to publications of the State Offices, arranged according to frequency of appearance within each State. Another handy source of information for publications issued by this Bureau is the *Yearbook of the Commonwealth of Australia*[166] which has been carrying for some years a chapter entitled "Statistical publications of Australia". Users of statistical data may also find some help through Palmer's *Guide to Australian economic statistics*[120a] to which reference has already been made. The second chapter of Palmer's *Guide* includes an extensive list of official statistical publications.

Though the Bureau of Agricultural Economics is an office of particular importance to Australia, there exists to date no index to the vital information contained in its reports and periodicals, but a list of them can be found in the Bureau's *Quarterly review of agricultural economics.*

The importance of the economic and industrial enquiries underlying the reports of the Tariff Board is unfortunately matched by the difficulty of tracing any particular item through the numerous and varied types of enquiries which have initiated these reports. The Research School of Pacific Studies of the Australian National University has issued as its first pamphlet in "Aids to Research Series" an *Index of Australian tariff reports, 1901-1961*[99a] which was compiled by G. J. R. Linge. The *Index* is based on a contents analysis of all tariff reports whether they are issued by Royal Commissions, Trade and Customs Inquiries or other bodies, and it lists each report within a main industry group or sub-group. The reference to each subject clearly states the type of enquiry where the tariff was discussed, the date of the report and the Parliamentary Paper where it was printed. There is also a list of Tariff Board reports not printed as Parliamentary Papers and a finding list for the Board's Annual Reports.

Some efforts have been made to approach the bibliography of government publications through lists of reports which are the results of certain types of governmental processes. The importance of public inquiries has been recognized for centuries as an essential part of democratic government, and in the British Commonwealth their reports have usually been public documents, accessible to the community at large. A. H. Cole compiled a *Finding list of Royal commission reports in the British dominions, 1939,*[64] which contains entries for Australian Royal commissions on pp. 15-86. The entries are arranged chronologically according to states. While for some unaccountable reason the personal name of the Government Printer is given for each report, the name of the chairman is only rarely shown. An attempt to provide an exhaustive list of Australian Royal commissions and similar public hearings is being made by D. H. Borchardt in his *Check list of Royal commissions, select committees of Parliament and boards of inquiry*,[54] of which two parts only have appeared so far, as part of W. Stone's series *Studies in Australian bibliography* (nos 7 and 10). The first of these deals with the Commonwealth of *Australia, 1900-1950*, 1958, the second with *Tasmania 1856-1959*, 1960. Both provide the names of all commissioners sitting on each inquiry and a synopsis of the recommendations, but it should be noted that the Tasmanian volume does not include the reports of Selected Committees of Pariament for reasons set out in the introduction.

VII

BIBLIOGRAPHY IN AUSTRALIA

(a) A Brief Moral Discourse on Bibliography

As a subject of scholarly endeavour bibliography has been developed only fairly recently in Australia. A mere glance at the publication date of the majority of titles mentioned in this book shows clearly that few bibliographies have been compiled or published in Australia before the 1920's, and that there has been no real progress in this field until after the Second World War. This is not surprising, since from a merely practical point of view bibliographies can only be compiled in the presence of substantial collections of books and journals. Until the beginning of the twentieth century there existed in Australia only three libraries of reasonable size: The Public Libraries of New South Wales and of Victoria, and the Fisher Library of the University of Sydney. Besides, there had been formed two large private collections — the Mitchell and the Petherick collections — but of these the latter remained in the owner's hands until 1911. At the outbreak of World War II, some other of the state and university libraries had grown into fairly useful collections, and the National Library of Australia had formed a basic book stock which began to play its part in the bibliographic resources of the country. To these was also added the far-flung, but well organized, stock of the CSIRO libraries. Even today the total bibliographic wealth of Australia's leading research libraries is estimated to be about 10 million books, scarcely more than the holdings of a single one of the large national collections of the northern hemisphere.

But neither books alone, nor buildings to house them, make a library. A number of famous men have made statements on books which have been handed down from generation to generation like some piece of holy writ. Yet time has proved these statements to be at least inadequate and some of the most famous ones have been found to be empty words. Whatever Carlyle may have had in mind when he shouted to the world his dictum "A true university is a collection of books" — his sobering experience *vis-à-vis* the winds of reform that were blowing through the British Museum only shows that books alone do not make a university. The millions spent by Andrew Carnegie in the form of capital grants on the building and stocking of libraries in the English-speaking world were often wasted because no provision was made for staffing and maintaining them. In Australia, not only Carnegie foundations of the early twentieth century, but also many more recent libraries have suffered the frustrating experience of having reasonably equipped buildings, sometimes reasonable book votes, but rarely if ever adequate trained staff. Buildings, books and bibliothecaries — these three have to be together in a just proportion to make libraries and librarianship possible. It may be appropriate, at this point, to define briefly what the aims of librarianship are and then to look at the Australian achievements in this field.

There are schools of thought in which there is much talk about the "Philosophy of Librarianship". There are others whose view of the library profession and its place in life is not only strictly empirical but also thoroughly pragmatic. To them the quintessence of their calling is the sombre and heraldic "ich dien". Since Australia is historically tied to the one and emotionally bound up with the other, it may well be right and proper that an Australian approach to the profession of librarianship should be independent, could be new, but at any rate must be constructive. Indeed, it seems to me that if we add to the three-dimensional basis of librarianship — buildings, books and bibliothecaries — that fourth dimension which alone justifies the existence of the other three — borrowers, we are immediately presented with a harmonious geometric form, which is flexible and presents different values as any one factor in the formation changes.

At this point, it becomes us to halt for a moment since a new concept has been introduced, the concept of value. What values are there in the four biblio-dimensions? During the past 5000 years or more of recorded human history, the very fact that it has been recorded has been considered a thing of value. This value is not an absolute measure, a thing in itself — it is a relative value, dependent on nothing else but emotional and educational factors. But to the extent that it has been universally so recognized, i.e., that all men appear to have held cognizance of the past as valuable, we may be permitted to say quite simply that the transmission in permanent form of the cognizance of the past is of value. From the recognition of this value sprang the book; not in a day, a month or a year, as is so often imagined even by some who ought to know better – but during centuries of development. The book, then, as an abstract concept, has a value which distinguishes it from other things and which at the same time makes it the origin for the four-dimensional biblio-system.

The book is and will remain the heart and essence of librarianship. New ideas and developments in methods of communication are supposed to have threatened the place which the book has held for so long – the book in its varied but essentially standard forms which developed from the hewn-stone inscriptions of yore to the microfilm of today. Indeed, many public librarians in a misguided effort to justify their existence have of late more than ever before tried to assure the world that the present and future development of improved means of communication do not and will not (presumably by historical analogy) detrimentally affect the consumption of "good" books. They are wrong, not because of any serious fault in their argument nor even in their conclusion, but because they are reasoning from a false premise. Librarians do not have to justify their existence – they exist.

This is not the place to consider at length the universal importance of the library profession, a profession as old as the written records of man. What I wish to define and emphasize is the equally basic notion that librarianship is naught without the written word, just as we well know that the written word would have perished without librarianship. The book is the sum, and its preservation and utilization the object, of librarianship. This definition is not affected by the admission that there are books of various kinds, some useful to my eyes and others harmful to the eyes of my neighbour. Differences of contents are not a subject under discussion. Any doubts that may exist on the score can and must be dispelled by the admission that every book is a brainchild of some author, and as such it is a reflection of some part of mankind, however small, however insignificant; good or bad are but relative terms, affected by space and time and differing from one generation to another.

It is not the librarian's task to make other people read, and still less to make them read what the librarian may consider good for them. Much has been said on the educational function of libraries and of the didactic tasks of librarians, but the arguments are not yet altogether convincing. A librarian's contribution to the complex system of national education is entirely different from that of the schoolmaster or any other person trained to stand before a group and to lecture or to lead discussions. The librarian's function is essentially descriptive in character; he collects and describes what he has collected for the benefit of others, so that they may find their way more easily through the mass of documents — written, printed, photographed, etc., etc. — which they need or think they need for their enlightenment and for the progress of mankind — or maybe even for mere survival.

It is not suggested that teaching in the accepted sense and librarianship are incompatible. We find architects who are expert practical plumbers and we find surgeons who are outstanding historians of medicine. But these are extraordinary people, and the combination of such talents is rare; we also find librarians who are great teachers or leaders of adult education groups, but it is unreasonable to expect all librarians to be gifted in this way, simply because librarianship is essentially different from education-group-leadership and from class teaching. If librarianship is to be ranged among any of the larger groups of organized knowledge, it can only be classed as a descriptive science. That is its true function and its *raison d'être*.

Librarianship is held by many to be divisible into various sorts of classes or sections according to the clientele which it serves. Accordingly, there is supposed to be some critical difference between librarians operating in libraries for children and those who have only adults as readers, between those who work with groups of specialists and those who assist a heterogeneous group of university students and staffs. Yet when we look at their basic tasks these appear to be remarkably alike: whether the printed matter collected is to be used by minds as yet innocent of good and evil or whether it is to be exploited to satisfy Mammon, whether it is to be used to sharpen the wits of some future musical or mathematical genius or whether, last but not least, it is to help some poor and tired spirit to while away the lonely hours of the night — all want the librarian to help them find what they are looking for. Bibliography is the description of books, and the purpose of description is surely to help those who are searching among a mass of similar objects to find the one they really want. It matters naught who searches. The intrinsic value of the descriptive process is not affected by the searcher's level of intellectual aspiration or by his social class. For that reason the process of description is independent of the subject described and there is in it, on the face of things, no value judgment. Librarianship seen in this light is purely and simply a bibliographic task. The recognition of this fact does not deny that there are many facets of bibliography which require years of study and wide experience before they can be carried out with any degree of competence, nor is it asserted that the bibliographic nature of librarianship is an auxiliary occupation as has often been assumed in the past. The description of books is a justified end in itself, which requires specialized knowledge peculiar to the profession of librarianship.

(b) Australian Bibliographic Work

It has already been stated that the Australian achievement in the field of bibliography is not as yet very great, and it must be owned that its history is marked by tombstones which reflect an abnormally high rate of infant mortality. However, this is not the place to probe into the causes and reasons for this partial failure, and as a fit conclusion to this survey it is more appropriate to review briefly the kind of work that is being done in Australia in areas of knowledge not always directly linked with the subject "Australia". One can distinguish quite generally between two types of bibliographical activity: one is part of the professional processes carried out in libraries, the other is practised by enthusiasts both amateur and professional. The former is perhaps best termed institutional bibliography and the other private bibliography.

A. Institutional Bibliography

Foremost in importance is without doubt the effort of the National Library of Australia to compile and maintain a union catalogue of monographs held in the major libraries of the Commonwealth. About 35 libraries are co-operating in the project which at the time of writing is still rather in its infancy. Since 1960 the co-operating libraries have sent entries for books received after 1 January 1960 to the National Union Catalogue and the whole card catalogue of one library has been filmed and the film reproduced on cards by means of copy-flow. The project is at this stage divided into two sections: the maintenance and possible publication in book form of an *Australian union catalogue of current monograph accessions* and the publication in book form of a *Retrospective union catalogue of monographs in Australian libraries.* The National Library of Australia is being advised in this huge project by the Australian Advisory Council on Bibliographical Services.

The most advanced union cataloguing project in Australia is the union list of scientific periodicals which the CSIRO is sponsoring under the simple title *Scientific serials in Australian libraries.*[131] This important and highly successful work was begun as long ago as 1930 when E. R. Pitt brought out the first edition of the *Catalogue of scientific and technical periodicals in libraries of Australia.* A *Supplement* was edited by C. A. McCallum and D. W. I. Cannan and published in 1934. In 1944 E. R. Pitt was commissioned to bring out a new and revised edition, which was published in 1951 as the *Union catalogue of the scientific and technical periodicals in the libraries of Australia;* this 2nd edition was also augmented by a *Supplement* covering the years 1946-1952 and edited by Adelaide L. Kent. To this point, the production of this important reference tool remained within the bounds of standard bibliographic and publishing practice. However, as Australian libraries developed and increased their bibliographic resources, the publication of union lists in book form was becoming less and less practicable and their usefulness more questionable. The CSIRO decided therefore to begin a new type of union catalogue which would combine the advantages of the old sheaf catalogue with those of the printed book catalogue. The result of the marriage was *Scientific serials in Australian libraries,* issued in 1960 in loose-leaf form under the editorship of Jean A. Conochie. Stout screw binders were issued as part of the union catalogue and its over 1,700 pages list today more than 10,000 serials held in over 300 libraries. Replacement sheets containing new and amended entries are sent out at least once a year.

While periodicals in the fields of science and technology have thus been well cared for, those in the humanities and social sciences are only just beginning to receive the attention they deserve. A *Union catalogue of periodicals in the social sciences and the humanities,* held in Australian libraries, has been kept on cards for more than 20 years in the Australian National Library. On the insistence of AACOBS steps were taken in 1963 to follow the pattern set by CSIRO for *Scientific serials in Australian libraries* and as a first instalment a pilot list was issued in 1963

65

under the title *Serials in Australian libraries, social sciences and humanities, a union list*. This union list covers periodicals and other serials in the subjects indicated by the title, but newspapers, company reports and minor publications of mainly local interest are excluded. The editor, R. Kaspiew, aware of the shortcomings of the pilot list, proceeded at once with the preparations of the loose-leaf edition which began its appearance in 1964.[132a] At the time of writing entries falling into the first three letters of the alphabet have been issued in loose-leaf form and work on the remainder is proceeding, albeit slowly. It is expected that when completed SALSSH will contain about 30,000 entries and the same arrangements have been made for its maintenance and current upkeep as for SSAL.

The two main lists, SSAL and SALSSH are complementary and except for a very small number of titles of interest to all kinds of research workers, there is no duplication of effort. However, in view of the constantly changing directions of scholarly and scientific endeavours any one looking in vain for a title in one union list may hope to find it in the other, and it is therefore necessary for all research libraries to subscribe to both union lists.

AACOBS also sponsored the publication of a brief list of the principal bibliographies and bibliographic services likely to be most used in local libraries in Australia. The booklet appeared for the first time in 1961 under the title *Bibliographies and bibliographical service for Australian public libraries*.[34a] Its 60 titles are divided into three sections according to the size of public library service for which they would be most suitable. A list of this type is essential where there is a dearth of professionally trained librarians and to this end all entries are annotated, showing the purpose of the item described, its cost as well as address of publisher.

Regional union lists of periodicals are maintained on cards in the University of Tasmania Library and in the State Library of Western Australia, and some branches and divisions of the Library Association of Australia have sponsored the publication of regional union lists. These latter are short-title lists and some of them are only of limited usefulness because they do not indicate the extent of holdings. Nevertheless they are all signs of the growing consciousness that Australia's bibliographic resources are so slender that co-operation is imperative.

The development of special collections within a library often brings in its train the desire to record such wealth or specialty in book form. Typical examples of this type of bibliography are the catalogues of early books in the State Library of Victoria. A. B. Foxcroft compiled both of them, one *A catalogue of English books and fragments from 1477 to 1535 in the Public Library of Victoria,* 1933,[158] and the other *Catalogue of fifteenth century books and fragments in the Public Library of Victoria,* 1936.[159]

Similarly, anniversaries and ceremonial occasions prompt the publication of bibliographic catalogues as for instance G. A. Farmer's *A check list of the collected editions of the works of William Shakespeare held in the major Australian libraries,* 1964.[80a] Though a useful list, its simplicity and homely appearance is scarcely in keeping with the occasion and the significance of the exhibition. A more impressive catalogue was issued by the Public Library of New South Wales as *An exhibition in commemoration of the 400th anniversary of the birth of William Shakespeare;*[113a] handsomely printed on glossy paper with facsimiles and other illustrations, the catalogue describes the largest collection of Shakespeareana in Australia. The entries are accompanied by useful annotations.

An interesting new development in cataloguing technique was used in the compilation of a union catalogue of certain sections of three of Melbourne's main libraries. Under the title *French culture in the libraries of Melbourne: The State Library of Victoria, Baillieu Library, University of Melbourne, Monash University Library,* 1962,[89e] the compilers R. Laufer, B. Southwell and W. Kirsop have brought together in one classified sequence the Gallicana holdings of the libraries listed. The catalogue has been set up with a photolist machine, and despite a number of serious shortcomings it is a pioneer enterprise which may lead to more efficient union cataloguing in Australia.

A good deal of bibliographic work is also being performed in general and special libraries of all kinds in response to requests from library users. Some of these bibliographies are published in one form or another, and made available to a wider field of readers. Thus the National Library, CSIRO libraries, the Public Library of South Australia and the State Library of Victoria — to name but four examples — issue frequently *ad hoc* bibliographies on a vast variety of subjects to meet requirements from research workers. Many of these bibliographies do not concern us in this present survey because they do not deal with Australia. However, they indicate that Australian librarianship has reached a level of competence which makes this type of service possible.

B. *Private Enterprise*

It is but natural that most of the privately organized bibliographic work should deal with Australian subject material. There is a natural stimulus, and the material is more or less at hand. Furthermore, the importance and the extent of the subject can be appreciated at a glance. Most of the work of this kind of any significance has been discussed in the preceding pages. There remains an area of bibliographical enterprise which is done for the sake of scholarship, for some particular utilitarian purpose, or in some rare cases just to satisfy a personal whim, and which — here is the point of difference — is not concerned with Australian subject matters. In the majority of cases this kind of bibliography is concerned with some subject in relation to Australia, a natural approach, since the environment provides in the last resort the impetus, and it would be well nigh impossible to embark on a bibliographic task for which the basic material is not even available in Australia.

Given the fact that the importance of early printed books is so widely recognized, it is surprising that a member of the staff of Auckland University should be the first to try to compile an inventory of seventeenth century English books in Australia. W. J. Cameron's *Short-title catalogue of books printed in Britain and British* [sic] *books printed abroad, 1641-1700, held in Australian libraries* ... 1962,[61] is the result of a brief visit to Australia at the end of 1960. The compiler claims that he has listed about 60 per cent of all books published in the period mentioned in the title, but close examination of the processes employed in extracting information from library catalogues would suggest that his estimate may be too high. Cameron's introduction and advice to librarians in Australia — and presumably elsewhere — is based on assumptions which I cannot share; as I have already written elsewhere,* it is regrettable that false values and unrealistic approaches to scholarship are often dominating attitudes to old books. Yet Cameron's basic list will remain a very useful starting point for future scholars.

* Australia's Wing [Review of W. J. Cameron's *Short-title catalogue* ...] in *Biblionews*, v15 no 2, 1962.

Personal interest has prompted the compilation of a *Union catalogue of library science periodicals in the major libraries of Australia*[55] in 1953 and its second edition in 1963. Another union list which grew as a by-product of other research work is P. N. Davis's *Finding list of American legal materials in Australian law libraries*, 1964.[70a] The usefulness of this *Finding list* would have been enhanced if the compiler had availed himself of professionally accepted symbols to indicate holding libraries instead of using his own system and adding a transliteration guide. The *Finding list* is arranged according to the hierarchy of the institutions in the U.S.A. The States materials are in the alphabetical order of the States, with separate sections for materials which are dealt with according to subject matter. There is almost endless scope for this type of work in all fields of interest, but within the limits of this survey it is not possible to offer programmes of work or directions for their execution.

A work not in any way related to Australia, but compiled in Hobart, Tas., is D. H. Tuck's *A handbook of science fiction and fantasy*.[154] Processed and published by the author first in 1957 and then in a revised edition of two volumes in 1959, this interesting compilation includes notes on authors and books, a title index and an index of publishers and numbered sequences. A third edition is about to appear under the imprint of an American publisher.

VIII

LIST OF WORKS REFERRED TO

This list contains entries for all works mentioned in the text with the exception of one or two which have not sufficient bibliographical value to justify their inclusion. The entries follow generally accepted library cataloguing rules and no distinction has been made between works printed by conventional means and those produced by some off-set process. Running numbers on the left refer from the text to the bibliographic entry; page references to the text are given on the right.

PAGE

1   ADAM, M. I. *Guide to the principal parliamentary papers relating to the Dominions, 1812-1911, by M. I. Adam [and others]* Edinburgh, Oliver & Boyd, 1913. (pp. 37-65).   54

ALLEN, G. G. see AUSTRALIA. COMMONWEALTH SCIENTIFIC AND INDUSTRIAL RESEARCH ORGANIZATION. SHEEP BIOLOGY LABORATORY.

2   AMERICAN GEOGRAPHICAL SOCIETY. *Research catalogue.* Boston, Hall, 1962. (15v and Atlas supplement) (v14: Australasia).   27

3   AMERICAN HISTORICAL ASSOCIATION. *Guide to historical literature. Board of editors: G. F. Howe [and others]* New York, Macmillan, 1961. (pp. 770-772: Australia . . . by A. D. Osborn).   25

4   ANDERSON, C. *Bibliography of Australian mineralogy.* Sydney, Government Printer, 1916. (New South Wales. Geological survey. *Mineral resources,* no 22).   40

5   ANDERSON, H. *Guide to ten Australian poets.* [Melbourne] Hawdon Davison, 1953.   46

70

List of Works Referred to

PAGE

6 ARGUS, Melbourne. *Index,* no 1-79, 1910-1949. Melbourne, Argus.　　17

7 ARNOT, J. F. *A bibliography of the newspapers filed in the Mitchell Library and the general reference collection of the Public Library of New South Wales.* Sydney, Public Library of New South Wales, 1944.　　15

8 AUSTRALIA. ARMY. ROYAL AUSTRALIAN SURVEY CORPS. *Catalogue of official military maps.* 2nd ed. Canberra, The Corps, 1962.　　27

9 — BUREAU OF AGRICULTURAL ECONOMICS. *Select bibliography of publications on Australian agricultural marketing, with comments on contents and character.* Canberra, The Bureau, 1957.　　32

9a — BUREAU OF METEOROLOGY. *List of publications, 1945 - 1960.* Melbourne, The Bureau, 1960.　　43

10 — COMMONWEALTH BUREAU OF CENSUS AND STATISTICS. *Publications, 1961- .* Canberra, The Bureau.　　57

— COMMONWEALTH NATIONAL LIBRARY see AUSTRALIA. NATIONAL LIBRARY.

11 — COMMONWEALTH OFFICE OF EDUCATION. *Educational research being undertaken in Australia, 1950- .* Sydney, The Office [1951]　　34

12 — COMMONWEALTH SCIENTIFIC & INDUSTRIAL RESEARCH ORGANIZATION. *Annual Report.* no 1- , 1926/7- . Canberra, Government Printer, 1927- .　　38, 57

12a — — *CSIRO published papers: Author index.* MELBOURNE, CSIRO, Head Office Library, 1964-1966.　　38

— See also Scientific serials on Australian libraries,

13 — — DIVISION OF FOREST PRODUCTS. *Bibliography on Australian timbers and other forest products, comp. by M. I. Hulme.* Melbourne, The Division, 1944.　　38

— — — — Supplement, no 1-3. Melbourne, The Division, 1945-1949.

14 — — — *Bibliography on eucalypts, 1956-61.* [Canberra, The Division, 1961]　　39

71

PAGE

15 — — — *Bibliography on the utilization of the eucalypts ... prepared for the FAO World Eucalypt Conference, Rome, 1956, by M. I. Hulme.* Melbourne, The Division, 1956.   39

15a — SHEEP BIOLOGY LABORATORY. *An Australian bibliography on original research on sheep and wool production, with special reference to the Merino, 1946-57, comp. by G. G. Allen.* Prospect, N.S.W., The Laboratory, 1958-1959. (Bibliography no. 1) 2 pts. (Pt. 2 has title: *An Australian bibliography on sheep and wool production*).   42

16 — DEPARTMENT OF EXTERNAL AFFAIRS. *Australian treaty list.* Canberra, Government printer, 1956. (Treaty series 1956, no. 1).   30

— — — Cumulative supplement (no. 2) 1962. (Treaty series 1962, no. 18).

17 — DEPARTMENT OF LABOUR AND NATIONAL SERVICE. *Bibliography of official Commonwealth and State publications relating to labour matters.* Melbourne, The Department, 1960.   33

— DEPARTMENT OF NATIONAL DEVELOPMENT. *Report ... on resources and development of the Murray Valley ...* see Murray Valley Resources Survey Committee.

18 — — RESOURCES INFORMATION AND DEVELOPMENT BRANCH. *Index to Australian resources maps of 1940-59.* Canberra, The Department, 1961.   26

19 — — DIVISION OF REGIONAL DEVELOPMENT. *A classified and selective bibliography on Australia for regional development purposes.* Canberra, The Division, 1948-1950. (8 pts. and Suppl. vol.).   39, 48

20 — — NATIONAL MAPPING OFFICE. *Map catalogue.* Canberra, The Office, 1955.   26

— — — — Amendment. no 1- , 1956- . Canberra, The Office.

21 — DEPARTMENT OF SOCIAL SERVICES. *Select bibliography on child welfare.* Canberra, The Department, 1955.   34

22 — — *Select bibliography on juvenile delinquency* [Melbourne, The Department, 1954]   34

PAGE

23 —   —   *Select bibliography on mental health* [Melbourne, The Department, 1955]   34

23a —   DEPARTMENT OF TERRITORIES. *Annotated bibliography of select government publications on Australian territories, 1951-1964.* Canberra, The Department, 1965.   51

24 —   DEPARTMENT OF THE NAVY. HYDROGRAPHIC SERVICE. *Catalogue and index of Australian charts and Admiralty charts of Australian waters.* Canberra, The Service, 1962.   27

24a —   FORESTRY AND TIMBER BUREAU. *Annual report,* no. 1- ; 1930-   . Canberra, The Bureau.   39

25 —   NATIONAL LIBRARY. *Annual catalogue of Australian publications.* no 1-25, 1936-1960. Canberra, The Library, 1937-1960.   11, 55

26 —   —   *Australian books, a select list,* 1933-   . Canberra, The Library, 1934-   . (To 1949 as *Select list of representative works dealing with Australia*).   12

27 —   —   *Banking in Australia, with special reference to the Commonwealth Bank and to banking legislation, 1911-1951.* Canberra, The Library, 1953. (Its *Select bibliographies. Australian series,* no 3).   32

28 —   —   *Books published in Australia, 1946-1960.* Canberra, The Library, 1946-1961.   11

29 —   —   *Checklist of serial publications of the Commonwealth of Australia.* Canberra, The Library, 1962.   56

30 —   —   *Conciliation and arbitration since 1947.* Canberra, The Library, 1952. (Its *Select bibliographies. Australian series,* no 1).   32

30a —   —   *Current Australian serials; a subject list, 1965.* Canberra, The Library, 1966.   13

30b —   —   *Guide to collections of manuscripts relating to Australia.* Canberra, The Library, 1964-   . (Loose-leaf)   26

31 —   —   *Mentally handicapped children . . . a select list compiled in co-operation with the Handicapped Children's Association (A.C.T.).* Canberra, The Library, 1958.   34

PAGE

32 — — *Select bibliography on economic and social conditions in Australia, 1918-1953.* Canberra, The Library, 1953.　31

33 — — *Select list of bibliographical publications relating to Australia* [Canberra, The Library, 1951]　8

— — *Select list of representative works dealing with Australia* see Its *Australian books.*

— — see also *Australian government publications; Australian national bibliography; Serials in Australian libraries.*

34 — — AUSTRALIAN BIBLIOGRAPHICAL CENTRE. *Australian bibliography and bibliographical services.* Canberra, Australian Advisory Council on Bibliographical Services, 1960.　7

34a — — — *Bibliographies and bibliographical services for Australian public libraries.* Canberra, The Centre, 1961.　66

34b — — — *National bibliographical services and related activities . . . Australia.* 1961- . Canberra, The Centre.　7

35 — — — *Union list of newspapers in Australian libraries.* Canberra, Australian Advisory Council on Bibliographical Services, 1959-1960. (2 pts.).　16

— — — — Supplement.

— NATIONAL MAPPING OFFICE see AUSTRALIA. DEPARTMENT OF NATIONAL DEVELOPMENT. NATIONAL MAPPING OFFICE.

36 — PARLIAMENT. *First consolidated index to the papers presented to Parliament, 1901-1949.* Canberra, Government Printer, 1955.　55

36a — *Australian books in print,* 1955- . Melbourne, Thorpe. (Biennial)　13

37 AUSTRALIAN COUNCIL FOR EDUCATIONAL RESEARCH. *Theses in education and educational psychology accepted for degrees in Australian universities, 1919-1950.* Melbourne, The Council, 1953.　34

— — Supplement, 1951 to 1953. Melbourne, 1955.

List of Works Referred to

PAGE

38 *Australian education index.* vl- , 1957- . Melbourne, Australian Council for Educational Research, 1958- .   34

39 *Australian geographer.* vl- , 1928- . Sydney, Geographical Society of New South Wales.   26

40 *Australian geographical record.* no 1- , 1959- . Canberra, Institute of Australian Geographers.   26

41 *Australian government publications.* vl- , 1961- . Canberra, National Library of Australia, 1962- . (Issued annually).   12, 56

42 — vl-8, 1952-1960. Canberra, Commonwealth National Library. (Issued monthly and cumulated in the Library's *Annual catalogue of Australian publications*).   56

42a AUSTRALIAN INSTITUTE OF ABORIGINAL STUDIES. *Bibliography, series A: selected periods,* no 1- , 1962- . [Canberra, The Institute]   36

43 *Australian journal of social issues.* vl- , 1961- . Sydney, Committee for Post-graduate Study in Social Work.   33

43a *Australian literary studies.* vl- , 1963- . Hobart, University of Tasmania.   47

44 *Australian national bibliography.* vl- , 1961- . Canberra, National Library of Australia, 1962- .   11, 12

45 *Australian periodical index,* 1956-1964. Sydney, Public Library of New South Wales, 1957-1964.   19

46 *Australian public affairs information service.* no 1- , 1945- . Canberra, National Library of Australia.   13, 19

47 *Australian science abstracts.* vl-35 no 5, 1922-1957. Sydney, Australian and New Zealand Association for the Advancement of Science. (From vl7 to v35 issued with the *Australian journal of science.*)   37

48 *Australian science index.* vl- , 1957- . Melbourne, Commonwealth Scientific and Industrial Research Organization.   13, 37

49 *Australian social science abstracts.* no 1-18, 1946-1954. Melbourne, Social Science Research Council of Australia.   19

PAGE

50 BARNARD, A. *The Australian wool market,* 1840-1900. Melbourne, Melbourne University Press [1958] (pp. 207-214). 32

50a BEAGLEHOLE, J. C. *The exploration of the Pacific.* London, Black, 1934. 21

51 *Bibliographie cartographique internationale.* vl- , 1946- . Paris, Colin, 1949- . 26

52 *Biblionews.* no 1- , 1947- . Sydney, Book Collectors' Society of Australia. 45

BLAKESLEE, G. M. see DUTCHER, G.M.

BLUETT, A. R. see BROWNING, R. J.

53 BORCHARDT, D. H. *Australian bibliography: an assay.* In *College and research libraries,* v23 : 207-212, 251-254, 1962). 8

54 — *Check list of Royal commissions, select committees of Parliament and boards of inquiry.* Cremorne, N.S.W., Stone Copying Co. 1958- . (Pt. 1, Commonwealth of Australia, 1900-1950; Pt. 2, Tasmania, 1856-1959) (*Studies in Australian bibliography,* no 7 and 10). 58

55 — *Union list of periodicals on library science and bibliography, comp. by D. H. Borchardt and P. K. Patil.* Hobart, University of Tasmania, 1963. 69

55a BORRIE, W. D. *The assimilation of immigrants in Australia and New Zealand; an annotated bibliography, by W. D. Borrie assisted by D. R. G. Packer.* [Canberra] Department of Demography, Research School of Social Sciences, Australian National University [1953] 33

56 BROSSES, C. de. *Histoire des navigations aux terres australes* . . . Paris, Durand, 1756. (2v). 21

57 BROWNING, R. J. *A digest of Australian cases relating to local government, reported up to the end of 1918, by R. J. Browning and A. R. Bluett.* Sydney, Law Book Co., 1919. 30

57a BRYAN, H. *Australian university libraries today and tomorrow.* Sydney, Bennett, 1965. 34

58 BUTLIN, S. J. *Foundations of the Australian monetary system, 1788-1851.* Melbourne, Melbourne University Press [1952] (pp. 555 - 573). 31

PAGE

59 *C.S.I.R.O. Abstracts.* v1- , 1952- . Melbourne,
    Commonwealth Scientific and Industrial Research
    Organization.   38

59a CAIDEN, N. *A bibliography for Australian universi-
    ties.* (In V*estes,* v6 no 3 and 4, 1963; v7 no 2, 3 and
    4, 1964; v8 no 1, 1965).   35

60 *Cambridge history of the British Empire.* Cambridge,
    University Press, 1929-1959. 8v. (v7 Pt. 1: Australia
    (pp. 645-712)).   23, 53

61 CAMERON, W. J. *A short-title catalogue of books
    printed in Britain and British books printed
    abroad, 1641-1700, held in Australian libraries,
    with an introduction by W. J. Cameron on the
    development of rare book collections and research
    facilities in Australian and New Zealand libraries.*
    Sydney, Wentworth Press, 1962. (*Studies in Aus-
    tralian bibliography,* no 11).   68

62 CENTRAL MEDICAL LIBRARY ORGANIZA-
    TION, Melbourne. *Author index to selected Aus-
    tralian medical periodicals.* 1955- . Melbourne,
    The Organization, 1956- .   41

63 CLARK, C. M. H. *A history of Australia.* Melbourne,
    Melbourne University Press [1962-] (v1 : 389-410).   24

63a COFFEY, W. G. *A bibliography of the Hunter
    Valley region, New South Wales.* Newcastle,
    N.S.W., Hunter Valley Research Foundation, 1964.
    (Hunter Valley Research Foundation Monograph
    no 19).   49

64 COLE, A. H. *Finding-list of Royal commission re-
    ports in the British dominions.* Cambridge, Mass.,
    Harvard University Press, 1939. (pp. 15-86).   58

    COMMONWEALTH FORESTRY AND TIMBER BUREAU see
    AUSTRALIA. FORESTRY AND TIMBER BUREAU.

64a *Commonwealth publications,* no 1- ; 1965- .
    Canberra, Commonwealth Government Printing
    Office. (Monthly and consolidated, irregular, lists).   56

    COOKE, T. F. see VICTORIA. STATE LIBRARY.
    Classified catalogue of Australiana.

    COOPER, C. F. see VICTORIA. SOIL CONSERVATION
    AUTHORITY.

PAGE

65 COULLS, A. *Bibliography of books, pamphlets, maps, etc., on Broken Hill and district.* 4th ed. Broken Hill, Council of the City of Broken Hill, 1965. 52

66 CRAIG, J. *Bibliography of public administration in Australia (1850-1947), with an introduction by T. H. Kewley* [Sydney] Dept. of Government and Public Administration, University of Sydney, 1955. 28

66a CRISP, L. F. *Australian national government* [Melbourne] Longmans [1965] (Select bibliography, pp. 455-470). 29

67 CROWLEY, F. K. *The records of Western Australia.* Perth, University of Western Australia, 1953. (Pt. 1, all published to date). 51

68 CULEY, A. G. *Bibliography of beef production in Australia (c.1930-1958).* Sydney, Division of Animal Health, McMaster Animal Health Laboratory, Commonwealth Scientific and Industrial Research Organization, 1961. 42

68a CURRIE, J. L. *A catalogue of books on Australia and neighbouring colonies, being a portion of the library of John L. Currie of Lawarra (formerly Larra).* Melbourne, Walker, May, 1885. 6

68b CUTHBERT, E. I. *Index of Australian and New Zealand poetry.* New York, Scarecrow Press, 1963. 45

69 DAVEY, L. *CSIRO water research bibliography, 1923-1963* [Melbourne] CSIRO, 1964. 43

70 DAVID, Sir T. W. E. *The geology of the Commonwealth of Australia, ed. and much supplemented by W. R. Browne.* London, Arnold, 1950. (3v) (Extensive bibliographies at end of chapters). 40

70a DAVIS, P. N. *Finding list of American legal materials in Australian law libraries; with foreword by the Attorney-General of the Commonwealth of Australia, the Honorable B. M. Snedden, M.P.* [Canberra, Australian National University, 1964] 69

71 DAVIS, S. R. *The literature of Australian government and politics, by S. R. Davis and C. A. Hughes.* (In *Australian journal of politics and history,* v4:107-133, 1958). 29

PAGE

DAVIS, S. R. see also LIVINGSTON, W. S.

71a DORNBUSH, C. E. *Australian military bibliography.* Cornwallville, N.Y., Hope Farm Press, 1963.   25

DUNN, E. J. see VICTORIA. DEPARTMENT OF MINES.

71b DU RIETZ, R. *Captain James Cook; a bibliography of literature printed in Sweden before 1819.* Uppsala, 1960.   23

72 DUTCHER, G. M. *Guide to historical literature.* New York, Macmillan, 1931. (Section V pp. 957-962 by G. M. Blakeslee).   25

73 DWYER, C. F. *Periodicals in education, psychology and related subjects in Melbourne libraries: a list* [2nd ed.] Melbourne, Australian Council for Educational Research Library, 1954.   34

74 EDWARDS, Francis Ltd. *Australasian catalogue; catalogue of books relating to Australasia, Malaysia, Polynesia, the Pacific coast of America, and the South Seas ...* London, Edwards, 1899. (The firm has issued many similar catalogues; the most noteworthy ones in this context appeared in 1928, 1934 and 1936).   4

75 ELLIS, M. H. *Lachlan Macquarie, his life, adventures and times, with reference notes and bibliography.* Sydney, Dymock, 1947. (pp. 596-605).   24

76 ELLIS, U. R. *Australian new states movement: bibliography* [Canberra, Office of Rural Research, 1956]   29

77 — *Bibliography [of the] Australian Country Party (Federal)* [Canberra, The Author, 1956]   29

78 — *Bibliography [of the] Australian Country Party* (N.S.W.). Canberra [The Author] 1956.   29

79 ETHERIDGE, R. *Catalogue of works, papers, reports and maps on the geology, palaeontology, mineralogy, mining and metallurgy, etc., of the Australian continent and Tasmania, by R. Etheridge and R. L. Jack.* London, Stanford, 1881.   40

80 FAIVRE, J. P. *L'expansion française dans le Pacifique de 1800 à 1842.* Paris, Nouvelles Editions Latines [1953] (pp. 505-530).   21

80a FARMER, G. A. *A checklist of the collected editions of the works of William Shakespeare held in the major Australian libraries.* Adelaide, Libraries Board of South Australia, 1964.   67

81 FERGUSON, Sir J. A. *Bibliography of Australia.* Sydney, Angus & Robertson, 1941- . (6v published to 1966).   8

82 FLINN, E. D. *The history, politics and economy of Tasmania in the literature, 1856-1959.* Hobart, University of Tasmania, 1961.   49

83 FOXCROFT, A. B. *The Australian catalogue; a reference index to the books and periodicals published and still current in the Commonwealth of Australia.* Melbourne, Whitcombe & Tombs, 1911. (Reprinted: London, Pordes, 1961).   9, 55

83a FRY, E. C. *Parliamentary papers . . . 1856-1900 as a source of labour history.* (In *Labour history,* nos 5, 6, 7, 8 and 10, 1963-1966).   33

84 GANDEVIA, B. H. *An annotated bibliography of the history of medicine in Australia; foreword by Sir Gordon Gordon-Taylor* [Sydney, Australasian Medical Pub. Co., 1957]   41

GANDEVIA, B. H. see also TOVELL, A.

85 GILL, T. *Bibliography of South Australia.* Adelaide [Government Printer] 1886.   50

85a — *Bibliography of the Northern Territory of South Australia [with supplements by C. H. Hannaford.* Adelaide, Public Library of South Australia, 1962] (*South Australian facsimile editions,* no 28).   51

86 GILSON, M. *Bibliography of the migrant press in Australia, 1847-1962.* 2nd draft. Canberra, Department of Demography, Australian National University, 1962.   16

87 GINSWICK, J. *A select bibliography of pamphlets on Australian economic and social history, 1830-1895.* Sydney, Law Book Co., 1961.   32

88 GIUSEPPI, M. S. *Guide to the manuscripts preserved in the Public Records Office.* London, HMSO, 1923-24. (2v).   54

PAGE

89 GRATTAN, C. H. *The United States and the South-west Pacific.* Melbourne, Oxford University Press, 1961. (pp. 253-266). 24

89a GREENWAY, J. *Bibliography of the Australian aborigines and the native peoples of Torres Strait to 1959* [Sydney] Angus & Robertson [1963] 36

90 GREENWOOD, G. *Australia; a social and political history.* Sydney, Angus & Robertson [1955] (pp. 418-427). 24

91 — *Brisbane, 1859-1959; a history of local government, by G. Greenwood and J. Laverty.* Brisbane, Ziegler for the Council of the City of Brisbane, [1959] (pp. 674-680). 52

92 — *The future of Australian federalism; a commentary on the working of the constitution* [Melbourne] Melbourne University Press, 1946. (pp. 310-316). 29

93 GROSS, A. *Attainment; being a critical study of the literature of federation, with bibliography.* Melbourne, Bread and Cheese Club, 1948. 23

93a HAWAII. UNIVERSITY. INDUSTRIAL RELATIONS CENTER. *Selected bibliographies on labour and industrial relations in Australia, India, Japan, New Zealand, Philippines.* Honolulu, The Center, 1961. 32

94 HEWITT, A. R. *Guide to resources for Commonwealth studies in London, Oxford and Cambridge, with bibliographical and other information.* London, Athlone Press, 1957. 5

95 *Historical studies, Australia and New Zealand,* v1- , 1940- . Melbourne, Melbourne University Press. 25

96 HOLDEN, W. S. *Australia goes to press.* Detroit, Wayne State University Press [1961] 14

97 HOLMES, Sir M. *Captain James Cook, R.N., F.R.S.; a bibliographical excursion.* London, Edwards, 1952. 22

98 HORNIBROOK, J. H. *Bibliography of Queensland verse, with biographical notes.* Brisbane, Government Printer, 1953. (Queensland. Library Board. *Publication,* no 1). 46

PAGE

HUGHES, C. A. see DAVIS, S. R., and LIVING-
STON, W. S.

HULME, M. I. see AUSTRALIA. CSIRO. DIVISION OF
FOREST PRODUCTS.

98a *Ideas about books and bookselling.* v1- , 1921-   .
Melbourne, Thorpe.   18

98b *Index to Australian book reviews.* v1- , 1965-   .
Adelaide, Libraries Board of South Australia.   20

JACK, R. L. see ETHERIDGE, R.

98c KELLY, C. *Calendar of documents; Spanish voyages
in the South Pacific from Alvaro de Mendaña to
Alejandro Malaspina, 1567-1794, and the Franciscan missionary plans for the peoples of the
Austral Lands, 1617-1794.* Compiled from manuscripts and other documents in the archives and
libraries of Spain, America, Rome, Paris, London,
Sydney, etc. Madrid, Franciscan Historical Studies,
in association with Archivo Ibero-Americano
(Madrid), 1965.   22

98d LANCASTER, H. O. *Bibliography of vital statistics
in Australia and New Zealand.* Sydney, Austral-
asian Medical Pub. Co., 1964.   42

98e LAUFER, R. *French culture in the libraries of Melbourne: The State Library of Victoria, Baillieu
Library, University of Melbourne, Monash University; comp. by Roger Laufer, Brian Southwell with
the assistance of Wallace Kirsop [Melbourne]
Monash University,* 1962-1963. (2v).   67

99   LEWIN, P. E. *A select list of recent publications
contained in the library of the Royal Colonial In-
stitute illustrating the constitutional relations be-
tween the various parts of the British Empire*
[London] Royal Colonial Institute, 1926.   30
—   *Subject catalogue of the library of the Royal
Empire Society.* see ROYAL COMMONWEALTH
SOCIETY.

99a LINGE, G. J. R. *Index of Australian tariff reports,
1901-1961.* Canberra, Australian National University, 1964. (Australian National University.
Research School of Pacific Studies. Aids to
research, A/1).   58

PAGE

99b LIVINGSTON, W. S. *Federalism in the Commonwealth; a bibliographical commentary.* London,
Cassell for the Mansford Society [1963] (pp.
29-57: *Federalism in Australia,* by S. R. Davis and
C. A. Hughes).   29

99c LOVEDAY, P. *Bibliography of selected manuscripts
relating to Australian politics since 1890 held in the
Mitchell Library, Sydney [by] Peter Loveday and
Helen Nelson* [Sydney] Department of Govern-
ment and Public Administration, University of
Sydney, 1964.   28, 49

     MACARTNEY, F. T. see MILLER, E. M. *Australian
literature . . . 1956.*

100 MACKANESS, G. *Annotated bibliography of Henry
Lawson.* Sydney, Angus & Robertson [1951]   46

101 — *The books of The Bulletin, 1880-1952; an annotated bibliography, by G. Mackaness and W. W.
Stone, with preliminary essays by W. E. Fitzhenry
and Norman Lindsay.* Sydney, Angus & Robertson
[1955]   45

102 McLAREN, I. F. *Australian aviation; a bibliographical survey* [Melbourne] Privately printed, 1958.   43

102a — *C. J. Dennis, his life and work.* Melbourne,
The Author, 1961.   46

102b — *Victorian Parliamentary papers relating to the
Aborigines* (in *Biblionews,* v10 no 9: 27-28,
1957).   35

     MAHONEY, D. J. see VICTORIA. DEPARTMENT OF
MINES.

103 MAIDEN, J. H. *The bibliography of Australian
economic botany.* Pt. 1. Sydney, Government
Printer, 1892. (Pt. 1, all published).   38

104 MAJOR, R. H. *Early voyages to Terra Australis now
called Australia; a collection of documents . . . from
the beginning of the sixteenth century to the time
of Captain Cook.* London, Hakluyt Society, 1859.   21

105 MARSHALL, M. J. *Union list of higher degree theses
in Australian university libraries.* Hobart, University of Tasmania Library, 1959.   14

PAGE

—   —   1st Supplement ... 1961.
—   —   2nd Supplement ... 1961.
—   —   3rd Supplement ... 1963.

105a MASSOLA, A. *Bibliography of printed literature upon Victorian aborigines.* (In Victoria National Museum. *Memoirs,* no 24, pp. 103-156, 1959).   36

106 MATHEWS, G. M. *Bibliography of the birds of Australia; books used in the preparation of this work [i.e., The birds of Australia] with a few biographical details of authors and collectors.* London, Witherby, 1925. (Issued as Supplements 4 and 5 of the author's *The birds of Australia*).   39

106a MAYER, H. *Bibliographical notes on the press in Australia.* Sydney, Dept. of Government and Public Administration, University of Sydney, 1963.   15

106b *Media guide and press directory of Australia and New Zealand.* 16th ed. Sydney, Country Press, 1964. (Cover title of 16th ed.: Press directory of Australia, New Zealand and the Pacific Islands).   15

107 MELBOURNE. UNIVERSITY. *Victorian historical documents* [Melbourne, 1949] (Pt. 1, An outline list of documents mainly in the Public Library of Victoria, and relating to the history of Victoria).   50

108 MILLER, E. M. *Australian literature from its beginning to 1935; a descriptive and bibliographic survey of books by Australian authors in poetry, drama, fiction, criticism and anthology, with subsidiary entries to 1938 ...* Melbourne, Melbourne University Press, 1940. (2v).   44

109 —   *Australian literature; a bibliography of 1938, extended to 1950; ed. with a historical outline and descriptive commentaries by Frederick T. Macartney.* Sydney, Angus & Robertson [1956]   44
MITCHELL LIBRARY, Sydney. see NEW SOUTH WALES. PUBLIC LIBRARY. MITCHELL LIBRARY.

110 MOORE-ROBINSON, J. *Chronological list of Tasmanian newspapers from 1810 to 1933* [Hobart, Monotone Art Printers] 1933.   16

PAGE

110a MURDOCH, A. *Bibliography of selected periodical articles on Australian economic subjects, published in English outside Australia, 1946-62.* (In *Economic record*, v 40, pp. 200-213, 1964.) ... 31

111 MURRAY VALLEY RESOURCES SURVEY COMMITTEE. *Report ... on resources and development of the Murray Valley.* Canberra, Department of National Development, 1947. (2v). (v1:346-356). ... 52

112 MUSGRAVE, A. *Bibliography of Australian entomology, 1775-1930; with biographical notes on authors and collectors.* Sydney, Royal Zoological Society of New South Wales, 1932. ... 39

NELSON, H. see LOVEDAY, P.

112a NEW SOUTH WALES. ARCHIVES AUTHORITY. *Guide to the state archives; list of series titles in the Archives Office of New South Wales.* Sydney, The Authority, 1965. ("... This list is preliminary"—Pref.) ... 49

112b — PUBLIC LIBRARY. *Abel Janszoon Tasman; a bibliography.* Sydney, Trustees of the Public Library, 1963. ... 22

113 — — *Australian bibliography ... catalogue of books in the Free Public Library, Sydney, relating to or published in Australia ...* Sydney, Government Printer, 1893. (3v in 1). ... 5

— — *Australian periodical index.* see *Australian periodical index.*

113a — — *An exhibition in commemoration of the 400th anniversary of the birth of William Shakespeare.* Sydney, The Library, 1964 ... 67

113b — — *Quiros memorials: a catalogue of memorials by Pedro Fernandez de Quiros, 1607-1615, in the Dixson and Mitchell Libraries, Sydney.* Sydney, The Library, 1961. ... 22

114 — — *Works on New South Wales; comp. at the Free Public Library, Sydney, under the direction of R. C. Walker ...* Sydney, Government Printer, 1878. ... 49

115 — — ARCHIVES DEPARTMENT. *Records of the Colonial Secretary of New South Wales ... Preliminary inventory.* Sydney, The Department, 1959-1960. 2 pts. (Pt. 1, Muster and census records; pt. 2, Naturalization and denization records, 1834-1904).   49

116 — — MITCHELL LIBRARY. *Bibliography of Captain James Cook ... comprising the collections in the Mitchell Library and General Reference Library, the private collections of William Dixson and J. A. Ferguson, and items of special interest in the National Library, Canberra, the Australasian Pioneers' Club, Sydney, and in the collection of the Kurnell Trust.* Sydney, Government Printer, 1928.   22

117 — — — *Index to periodicals, 1944-1959.* Sydney, The Library, 1950-1961. (4v).   19

118 — — — *Maps received in the Mitchell Library.* no 1- , 1958- . Sydney, The Library.   26

119 — — — *Selected list of reference books for Australasia and the Antarctic.* Sydney. [The Library] 1954.   8

119a — PARLIAMENT. LIBRARY. *Government documents in Australia; papers on their production, use and treatment* [Sydney] Joint Library Committee of the Parliament of N.S.W., 1965.   55

OSBORN, A. D. see AMERICAN HISTORICAL ASSOCIATION.

120 OVERACKER, L. *Publications on Australia useful to the political scientist: a selective survey.* (In American political science review. v47 : 844-857, 1953).   29

120a PALMER, G. *A guide to Australian economic statistics.* Melbourne, Macmillan, 1963. ("A survey of Australian statistical publications", pp. 15-37).   32

PATIL, P. K. see BORCHARDT, D. H. *Union list.*

121 PATON, Sir G. W. *The Commonwealth of Australia, the development of its laws and constitution.* London, Stevens, 1952. (pp. 327-333).   31

122 PETHERICK, E. A. *Bibliography of the State of Victoria, historical, descriptive, statistical.* (In Victorian historical magazine. v2-3, 1911/12-1912/13).   50

List of Works Referred to

—   *Catalogue of the York Gate Library* ... see
SILVER, S. W.

122a PILLING, A. R. *Aborigine culture history; a survey
of publications, 1954-1957.* Detroit, Wayne State
University Press, 1962.   36

122b *Pinpointer, a current subject index to popular periodicals.* vl- , 1963-   . Adelaide, Public Library
of South Australia.   19

123 POLITZER, L. L. *Bibliography of Dutch literature
on Australia.* Melbourne, The Author, 1953.   9

124 —   *Bibliography of French literature on Australia,
1595-1946.* Melbourne, The Author [1952]   9

125 —   *Bibliography of German literature on Australia,
1700-1947.* Melbourne, Pan Press, 1952.   9

126 POWER, G. W. *The Torrens Australasian digest,
being a digest of cases under the "Real Property"
(or Land Transfer) acts decided by the Supreme
Courts of the Australasian colonies, 1860-1898, together with comparative tables of those acts; comp.
by G. W. Power, Sir L. E. Groom and A. D.
Graham.* Brisbane, Queensland Law Journal, 1899.   25
*Press directory of Australia, New Zealand and Pacific
Islands* see *Media guide and press directory.*

127 QUICK, Sir J. *A classified catalogue of books and
writings by Australian authors.* Melbourne, Australian Literature Association [1927]   44

128 *Review of education in Australia.* vl- , 1938-   .
Melbourne, Australian Council for Educational Research.   34

129 ROBERTS, S. H. *History of Australian land settlement, 1788-1920; with an introduction by Ernest
Scott.* Melbourne, Macmillan, 1924 (pp. 402-421).   25

129a ROE, O. M. *Quest for authority in Eastern Australia,
1835-1851* [Melbourne] Melbourne University
Press [1965] (Bibliography, pp. 234-248).   29

130 ROYAL COMMONWEALTH SOCIETY. *Subject
catalogue of the library of the Royal Empire
Society, formerly Royal Colonial Institute, by
Evans Lewin* [London] The Society, 1930-1937.
(4v) (The sub-title of v2 is *The Commonwealth*

PAGE

of Australia, the Dominion of New Zealand, the South Pacific, general voyages and travels, and Arctic and Antarctic Regions, 1931).   4

131 *Scientific serials in Australian libraries, 1958-* . Melbourne, Commonwealth Scientific and Industrial Research Organisation. (Loose-leaf)   65

132 *A selected list of bibliographical aids covering the Pacific region, Australia and New Zealand.* [n.p., 1952?]   8

132a *Serials in Australian libraries, social sciences and humanities; a union list, 1964-* . Canberra, National Library of Australia. (Loose-leaf)   66

133 SERLE, P. *A bibliography of Australasian poetry and verse, Australia and New Zealand.* Melbourne, Melbourne University Press, 1925.   45

134 SKELTON, R. A. *Explorers' maps; chapters in the cartographic record of geographical discovery.* London, Routledge [1958]   26

135 SILVER, S. W. *Catalogue of the York Gate Library, formed by Mr. S. William Silver: an index to the literature of geography, maritime and inland discovery, commerce and colonization, by Edward Augustus Petherick.* 2nd ed. London, Murray, 1886.   3

136 SMITH, B. *Australian painting, 1788-1960.* Melbourne, Oxford University Press, 1962. (pp. 339-340).   47

137 — *European vision and the South Pacific, 1768-1850.* Melbourne, Oxford University Press, 1960. (pp. 258-274).   47

138 — *Place, taste and tradition; a study of Australian art since 1788.* Sydney, Ure Smith [1945] (pp. 274-275).   47

139 SOCIAL SCIENCE RESEARCH COUNCIL OF AUSTRALIA. *Bibliography of research in the social sciences in Australia, 1954-1957* [Canberra] The Council, 1958.   19

— *Bibliography of research in the social sciences in Australia, 1957-1960* [Canberra] The Council, 1961.

— *Australian social science abstracts* see *Australian social science abstracts.*

140 SOUTH AUSTRALIA. DEPARTMENT OF MINES AND GEOLOGICAL SURVEY. *Bibliography of South Australian geology; includes all literature published up to and including June 1958, by E. N. Teesedale-Smith.* Adelaide, The Department, 1959.   40

141 *South Australiana; a journal for the publication and study of South Australian historical and literary manuscripts.* no. 1- , 1962- . Adelaide, Public Library of South Australia.   51

142 SPENCE, S. A. *A bibliography of selected early books and pamphlets relating to Australia, 1610-1880.* London, The Author, 1952.   9
— — *Supplement to 1610-1880 (and extensions from) 1881-1900.* 1955.

143 — *Captain James Cook, R.N. (1728-1779); a bibliography of his voyages, to which is [sic] added other works relating to his life, conduct and nautical achievements.* Mitcham, Surrey, The Author, 1960.   23

144 SPRENT, P. *A research register of Australian mathematicians; comp. and ed. for the Australian Mathematical Society* [Hobart, University of Tasmania] 1958.   40

145 STEERE, F. G. *Bibliography of books, articles and pamphlets dealing with Western Australia issued since its discovery in 1616.* Perth, Government Printer, 1923.   51

145a STONE, G. *Australian science fiction index, 1939-1962.* Sydney, Futurian Society, 1964.   46
STONE, W. W. see *Biblionews;* MACKANESS, G. *The books of The Bulletin; Studies in Australian bibliography.*

146 STREIT, R. *Missionsliteratur von Australien und Ozeanien, 1525-1950, begonnen von R. Streit; fortgeführt von J. Dindinger.* Freiburg, Herder, 1955.   47

147 *Studies in Australian bibliography.* no 1- , 1954- . Cremorne, N.S.W. Stone Copying Co.   45

148 SWEET & MAXWELL LTD. London. *Legal biblio-graphy of the British Commonwealth of Nations.* 2nd ed. London, Sweet & Maxwell, 1958. (v6: *Australia, New Zealand and their dependencies from earliest times to June 1958 . . .*). 30

149 SYDNEY. TEACHERS' COLLEGE. *Education and related subjects: a list of periodicals in university, teachers' college and other education libraries in Australia.* Sydney, The College, 1951. 34

150 SYDNEY MORNING HERALD. *Index to the Sydney Morning Herald and the Sun-Herald.* no 1-139, 1927-1961. Sydney, Fairfax. (Includes index to the Sydney Mail to 1938 and Sunday Herald from 1949-1954). 17

151 TASMANIA. STATE ARCHIVES. *Guide to the public records of Tasmania, 1957-   .* Hobart, State Archives. (Sections 1, Colonial Secretary's Office record group; 2, Governor's Office record group; 3, Convict Department record group). 50

TEESEDALE-SMITH, E. N. *Bibliography of South Australian geology . . .* see SOUTH AUSTRALIA. DEPARTMENT OF MINES AND GEOLOGICAL SURVEY.

151a THORPE (D. W.) PTY. LTD. *Booksellers' reference book.* Melbourne, Thorpe, 1965. 14

152 THREADGILL, B. *South Australian land exploration, 1856 to 1880.* Adelaide, Board of Governors of the Public Library, Museum, and Art Gallery of South Australia, 1922. (2v) (v2: 170-179) 51

153 TOVELL, A. *References to Australia in British medical journals prior to 1880, by A. Tovell and B. Gandevia* [Melbourne, Museum of Medical History, Medical Society of Victoria] 1961. 41

153a TREGENZA, J. *Australian little magazines, 1923-1954; their role in forming and reflecting literary trends.* Adelaide, Libraries Board of South Australia, 1964. 15, 46

154 TUCK, D.H. *A handbook of science fiction and fantasy; a collection of material acting as a bibliographic survey to the fields of science fiction and fantasy (including weird), covering the maga-*

zines, books, pocket books, personalities, etc., of these fields up to December 1957. 2nd ed., rev. and enl. Hobart [The Author] 1959. (2v).   69

154a TURNBULL, C. *Kellyana.* Melbourne, Hawthorn Press, 1943.   25

155 UNITED STATES. LIBRARY OF CONGRESS. DIVISION OF BIBLIOGRAPHY. *A selected list of references on Australia, comp. by Grace Hadley Fuller under the direction of Florence S. Hellman.* Washington, The Library, 1942.   9

156 VICTORIA. DEPARTMENT OF MINES. *Biographical sketch of the founders of the Geological Survey of Victoria, with portraits by E. J. Dunn and bibliography by D. J. Mahoney.* Melbourne, Government Printer, 1910. (Its *Geological Survey Bulletin,* no 23).   40

157 — SOIL CONSERVATION AUTHORITY. *An annotated bibliography of the effects of fire on Australian vegetation, by Charles F. Cooper.* Melbourne, The Authority, 1963.   39

158 — STATE LIBRARY. *A catalogue of English books and fragments from 1477 to 1535 in the Public Library of Victoria, by A. B. Foxcroft, with preface by E. R. Pitt.* Melbourne, The Trustees of the Public Library, Museums, and National Gallery of Victoria, 1933.   67

159 — — *Catalogue of fifteenth century books and fragments in the Public Library of Victoria, comp. by Albert Broadbent Foxcroft, with a preface by E. R. Pitt.* Melbourne, The Trustees of the Public Library, Museums, and National Gallery of Victoria, 1936.   67

160 — — *Catalogue of the manuscripts, letters, documents, etc., in the private collection of the State Library of Victoria.* Melbourne, The Library, 1961.   50

161 — — *Classified catalogue of Australiana in the Public Lending Library of Victoria, by T. Fleming Cooke, with preface by E. R. Pitt.* Melbourne, The Trustees of the Public Library, Museums, and National Gallery of Victoria, 1936.   6

PAGE

161a *Victorian press manual and advertisers' handbook, containing an alphabetical list, with particulars of all newspapers published in the Colony of Victoria* . . . Melbourne, Moore & MacLeod, 1882.   15

162 WALKER, J. B. *List of books relating to Tasmania.* (In *Handbook for the use of members of the Australasian Association for the Advancement of Science, Hobart meeting, 1892.* Hobart, Government Printer, 1891, pp. 60-76).   49

162a WHEELWRIGHT, E. L. *Higher education in Australia.* Melbourne, Cheshire [1965] (pp. 337-408: *A bibliography for Australian universities,* by N. Caiden).   35

163 WHITTELL, H. M. *The literature of Australian birds: a history and a bibliography of Australian ornithology.* Perth, Paterson Brokensha, 1954.   39

164 WOODS, J. E. T. *Australian bibliography* (In *Australian monthly magazine,* v3: 161-166, 277-282, 1866).   2

165 WOODWARD, O. H. *A review of the Broken Hill lead-silver-zinc industry.* 2nd ed. Sydney, West Pub. Co., 1965. (Bibliography, pp. 491-512).   40

166 *Yearbook of the Commonwealth of Australia.* v 1- ; 1901/07-   . Canberra, Commonwealth Bureau of Census and Statistics, 1908-   . (see chapter "Statistical publications of Australia").   58

SUBJECT INDEX

Figures on the left of the subject term refer to the running number of the LIST OF WORKS REFERRED TO; page references to the text are given on the right.

42a, 89a, 102b, 105a, 122a   Aborigines, 35, 36

9   Agriculture, 32, 42, 43

30b, 112a, 115, 151, 160   Archives, 26, 49, 50

71a   Army, 25

136, 137, 138   Art, 47

77, 78   Australian Country Party, 29

23a   Australian Territories, 51

102   Aviation, 43

27   Banks and banking, 32

68   Beef production, 42

25, 26, 28, 33, 34, 34b, 36, 36a, 44, 53, 81, 83, 119, 132, 147, 151a, 155   Bibliography, 7, 8, 11, 12, 45, 55, 69

106, 163   Birds, 39

Boards of Inquiry see Royal Commissions

52   Book collecting, 45

98b   Book reviews — Indexes, 20

36a, 74, 151a   Booksellers' catalogues, 4, 13, 14

103   Botany, 38

91   Brisbane, 52

65, 165   Broken Hill, 52

101   Bulletin (The), 45

157   Bush fires, 39

21, 22, 31   Child welfare, 34

Commissions see Royal Commissions

94, 99   Commonwealth (British) 5, 30

71b, 97, 116, 143   Cook, James, 22, 23

10, 55a   Demography, 33, 57

102a   Dennis, C. J., 46

2, 50a, 56, 71b, 74, 80, 97, 98c, 104, 116, 135, 142, 143, 152   Discovery and exploration, 3, 4, 9, 21-23, 27, 51

123	Dutch literature on Australia, 9
61, 158, 159	Early printed books, 67, 68
32, 43, 83a, 87, 99a, 110a	Economic conditions, 31-33
19	Economic development, 48
11, 37, 38, 57a, 59a, 73, 128, 149, 162a	Education, 34, 35
112	Entomology, 39
14, 15	Eucalypts, 39
92, 93, 99b	Federalism, 23, 29
13, 14, 15, 24a, 157	Forestry and forests, 38, 39
98e	French language and literature, 67
80, 124	French literature on Australia, 9, 21
2, 8, 39, 40, 51	Geography, 26, 27
65, 79, 140, 156	Geology, 40
125	German literature on Australia, 9
66a, 71, 76, 77, 78, 92, 93, 94, 99b, 99c, 120, 129a	Government and politics, 5, 23, 28-30, 49, 50
1, 23a, 25, 29, 36, 41, 42 54, 64, 64a, 119a	Government publications, 11-13, 51, 53-59
3, 60, 63, 72, 87, 88, 90, 94, 95, 129	History, 5, 20-27, 32, 53
132a	Humanities, 66
63a	Hunter Valley, 49
55a	Immigration, 33
12, 59	Industrial research, 38, 57
16	International relations, 30
154a	Kelly gang, 25
17, 30, 83a, 93a	Labour, 32, 33
129	Land settlement, 25
57, 70a, 121, 126, 148	Law, 30, 31, 69
100	Lawson, Henry, 46
165	Lead mining, 40
57a	Libraries, 34
68a, 113, 130, 135, 161	Library catalogues, 3-6
5, 43a, 52, 68b, 98, 127, 133, 141, 145a, 153a	Literature, 15, 43-46, 51
57	Local government, 30
75	Macquarie, Lachlan, 24
30b, 88, 99c, 160	Manuscripts, 26, 28, 49, 50, 54
8, 18, 20, 24, 51, 118, 134	Maps, 26, 27
9	Marketing, 32

144   Mathematics, 40

62, 84, 153   Medicine, 41, 42

23, 31   Mental hygiene, 34

9a, 69   Meteorology, 43

71a   Military history, 25

4, 79   Mines and minerals, 40

98c, 146   Missions, Roman Catholic, 22, 47

58   Money, 31

98d   Mortality, 42

111   Murray River Valley, 52

18, 19   Natural resources, 26, 39, 48

114, 115   New South Wales, 49

76   New States Movement, 29

6, 7, 35, 86, 96, 106a, 106b, 110, 161a   Newspapers, 14-17

6, 150   Newspapers — Indexes, 17

23a, 85a   Northern Territory, 51

    Official publications *see* Government publications

5, 68b, 98, 133   Poetry, 45, 46

    Politics *see* Government and politics

    Press *see* Newspapers

73   Psychology, 34

57, 66   Public administration, 27-31

113b   Quiros, Pedro Fernandez de, 22

126   Real Property Acts, 25

146   Religion, 22, 47

54, 64   Royal Commissions, 58

12, 15a, 47, 48, 59, 131   Science, 36-43, 57, 65

145a, 154   Science fiction, 46, 69

29, 30a, 35, 73, 131, 132a, 153a   Serial publications, 13, 15, 16, 34, 46, 56, 65, 66

45, 46, 48, 98b, 117, 122b   Serial publications — Indexes, 13, 19, 20

80a, 113a   Shakespeare, William, 67

15a, 50   Sheep and wool, 32, 42

165   Silver mining, 40

32, 43, 83a, 87   Social conditions, 31-33

49, 132a, 139   Social sciences, 18-36, 65, 66

85, 141, 152   South Australia, 50, 51

98c   Spanish literature on Australia, 22

10, 98d, 120a, 166   Statistics, 32, 42, 57, 58

95

99a	Tariff reports, 59
112b	Tasman, Abel Janszoon, 22
82, 151, 162	Tasmania, 49, 50
105	Theses, 14
	Timber *see* Forestry and forests
126	Torrens system, 25
16	Treaties, 30
57a, 59a, 162a	Universities, 34, 35
122, 160	Victoria, 50
69	Water research, 43
67, 145	Western Australia, 51
	Wool *see* Sheep and wool
165	Zinc mining, 40